The ART of the BOARD

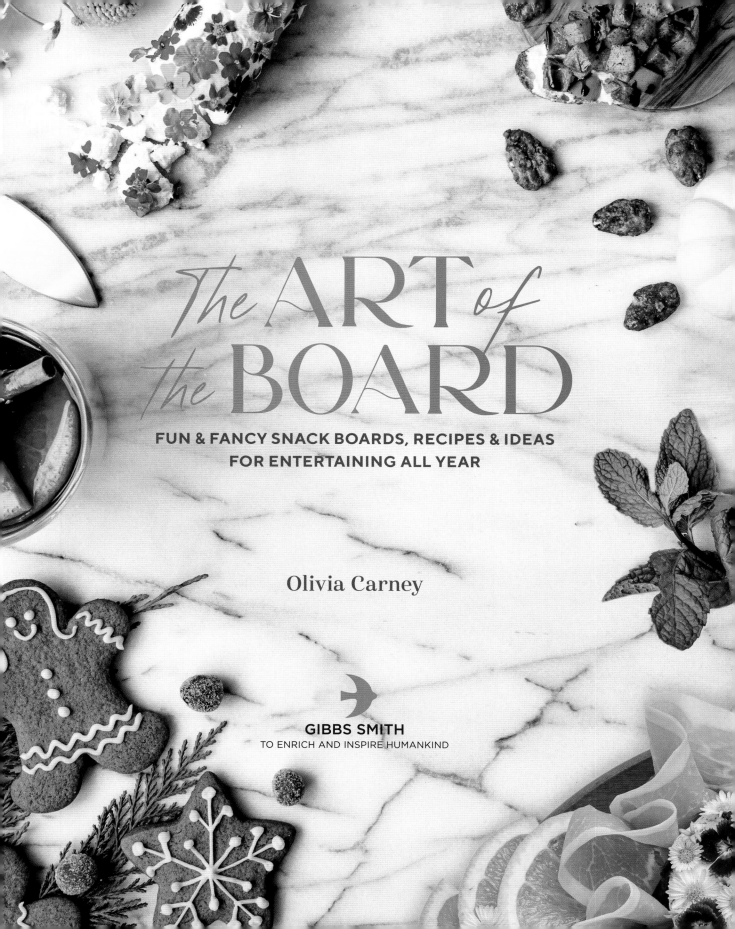

The ART of the BOARD

FUN & FANCY SNACK BOARDS, RECIPES & IDEAS
FOR ENTERTAINING ALL YEAR

Olivia Carney

GIBBS SMITH
TO ENRICH AND INSPIRE HUMANKIND

First Edition
26 25 24   8 7 6 5

Published by
Gibbs Smith
P.O. Box 667
Layton, Utah 84041

1.800.835.4993 orders
www.gibbs-smith.com

Designed by Gavin Motnyk
Photographs on pages ix, 1, 198, 214 by Kevin Morrissey
Illustrations by Victoria Carney

Editor: Gleni Bartels
Art director: Ryan Thomann
Production designer: Virginia Snow
Production manager: Felix Gregorio
Production editor: Sue Collier

Printed and bound in China

Gibbs Smith books are printed on either recycled, 100% post-consumer waste, FSC-certified papers or on paper produced from sustainable PEFC-certified forest/controlled wood source. Learn more at www.pefc.org.

Library of Congress Cataloging-in-Publication
Names: Carney, Olivia, author.
Title: The art of the board : fun & fancy snack boards, recipes & ideas for entertaining all year / Olivia Carney.
Description: First edition. | Layton, Utah : Gibbs Smith, [2022]
Identifiers: LCCN 2022005440 | ISBN 9781423661368 (hardcover) ISBN 9781423661375 (epub)
Subjects: LCSH: Snack foods. | LCGFT: Cookbooks.
Classification: LCC TX740 .C376 2022 | DDC 641.5/3—dc23/eng/20220215
LC record available at https://lccn.loc.gov/2022005440

To Chase, my forever partner
in life, for making all this possible.
Your patience, kindheartedness,
and support know no bounds.

CONTENTS

6: DIPS, SNACKS, COCKTAILS & MORE

HOPELESS HOSTESS

INTRODUCTION

O n Friday nights growing up, it was ritual for my family to sit down at our kitchen island and nosh on a cheese board together before heading out to dinner. Nothing fancy. My dad would peel open a block of Cooper Sharp American cheese, throw some banana peppers and a handful of pepperoni onto a wooden board, and grab a half-eaten bag of whole-grain crackers from the pantry. As we snacked on our little board of fridge-finds, we reminisced about our weeks, laughed at jokes pointed at each other, and enjoyed every minute spent around that island. While it may sound insignificant to some, the memories of those nights stay with me even to this day. Since then, I've always associated laughter, connection, and love with sitting around a platter of food. Sharing a meal together creates community and connectedness; it allows you to experience different cultures, build relationships, and find comfort in something so seemingly small. This is precisely why I've developed such a love for food boards. There's really no simpler–or foolproof–way to create lasting memories than to gather around a strikingly arranged spread and share moments (and cheese) together.

As I've gotten older, I've become more food-obsessed. I'd always dreamed of becoming a chef, and while that didn't exactly pan out (probably for the best–let's just say, handling stress isn't my strong suit), I've been given the gift of sharing my food creations with so many friends online. I started an Instagram account in the winter of 2019 to share my love of cheese boards with hopes that a few people might indulge me. Fast-forward just two years later, and I have hundreds of thousands of cheese-loving, charcuterie rose-making friends!

Sophia Loren once said, "Everything you see I owe to spaghetti." In my case, everything you see I owe to cheese (which includes this book and my stretchy pants). My family still laughs at the fact that a girl who once thought flour was an appropriate substitute for powdered sugar as a topping for brownies could have a food blog. And even though I persevered, no matter how much I worked to perfect my kitchen craft, after that incident I was forever deemed "hopeless" when it came to cooking, hosting, and nearly anything of the sort. So what have I decided to do? I'm leaning into that shit. I've written this book for the other "hopeless" hostesses and hosts out there who have the passion to entertain but maybe not the prowess (yet!). This is why throughout the book, you'll come across my scribbled Hopeless Hostess tips, which are essentially a peek into my brain. They're the tricks I've accumulated over the years that will make your boards really shine.

I like to think of my cheese and snack boards as my own works of art: The board is my canvas, the vivid ingredients are my paint, and my hands

are the brush. Sounds so tranquil, doesn't it? Well, for me, it's not—at least most of the time, anyway. While I would love to say that my process is full of serenity, it's not always peaceful. (Especially when I've taken a huge chunk off the side of my hand with a cheese grater, which has happened twice!) But even if the process is frantic, getting creative in the kitchen allows me to express myself through food. It's how I create food-inspired art, which is precisely why I named this book *The Art of the Board*.

In addition to detailing everything you'll need to plan and build unique cheese, charcuterie, and snack boards, I want to show you how to turn an everyday meal into an engaging experience for the people you're sharing it with. Food boards are tactile (which is a fancy way of saying they're an acceptable way to play with your food as a grown adult) and an immersive experience that brings people together. My only wish is that this book inspires you to carve out more time to enjoy the company of your family and friends and create lasting memories from small, intimate moments, just like the ones I had growing up.

Love and burrata,
Liv

1

THE ART
OF THE
BOARD

THE BUILDING BLOCKS OF A BOARD

L et's set a foundation before we jump into the actual board-making. In this section, we're talking about everything you need to get off on the right foot, including equipment, board components, the basics of assembly, and how you can successfully use this book to bring your vision to life! You can consider this section your go-to resource for board preparation. Then, a little later in the book, we will cover the extra tips and tricks that will take your board from being simply drool-worthy to "I can't even touch this because it's so damn beautiful!"

THE BOARD

It's the twenty-first century, and you know the drill: We eat with our eyes first, so finding the right foundation for your food is more important than you might think. First, let's consider the surface we'll use to serve our food. Boards come in many different shapes and dimensions, but there are a few standard sizes that are helpful to have on hand.

A standard rectangular board is 9 by 13 inches, and a standard circular board is typically 15 inches in diameter. Throughout the book you'll notice I use a variety of boards, depending on the occasion. For spreads meant to serve a smaller group,

I opt for a board smaller than the standard size. Or if the board has a lot of freely placed items (items that are placed directly on the board, not in ramekins), I choose one with raised edges to keep the food in place. It's important to consider both function and beauty when selecting a surface, but remember that the larger the board, the more expensive it will be to fill it!

Ultimately, your boards are an investment, so you'll want to take care of them. For detailed care instructions, take a look at Board Care 101 on page 186.

Wood

A wood board is like your favorite pair of flats: practical and reliable. I typically reach for a modern, minimalistic wood board that offers a bold grain and unique color, which keeps the spread from looking messy once a lot of the food is gone. I love the warmth that a wood board gives off. It's important that you choose a good-quality non-porous hardwood, which is relatively easy to maintain and lasts a long time.'

ACACIA: This wood has distinct graining with contrasting colors, making it one of the most popular and beautiful types of wood to use for snack boards. It's also very durable, so you won't need to worry about the damage from Aunt Judy digging her cheese knife aggressively into the Brie.

BAMBOO: An eco-friendly, durable, and surprisingly affordable option. Bamboo is not only remarkably sustainable but also stronger than most woods, which means that if you want your board to double as a cutting board, bamboo will hold up nicely.

CHERRY: Pick this if you're looking for rich, red undertones for your board. The grain is tighter and finer and has an even texture. Cherry one of the best all-around woods for regular wear and tear. However, it doesn't have any natural moisture protection, and direct sunlight can damage it if it's exposed for prolonged periods.

OLIVE: My personal favorite! Olive wood is incredibly beautiful, and with rich colors and uniquely fine-textured grain, it conveys a certain level of prestige. A creamy, golden wood with a very uniform pattern and color, olive is unmatched by other options. But beware—it's not for the faint of heart. Olive wood is much more expensive and has a lower durability than other woods, since it lacks necessary natural oils to protect its quality.

TEAK: This wood is environmentally friendly and known for its elegance and durability. It's water resistant and has an abundance of natural oils, which naturally protect its integrity. However, with its longevity and sustainability comes a higher price tag.

Marble

There is something about this natural stone that brings me so much joy. It's sleek and inviting, and it really adds an upscale sophistication to your board. Marble boards also photograph nicely, but you'll want to be careful to avoid ingredients that could stain—it happens quickly! Marble can be a bit pricey, too, so it's important to preserve its condition properly.

Slate

The dark gray color of slate contrasts beautifully with the vibrant colors of cheeses, fruits, and charcuterie. A slate board also allows for a bit of fun and creativity. Since its surface is like a chalkboard, you can easily decorate, illustrate, or label all your offerings—so your friends who aren't fond of stinky cheese don't reach for the Camembert. I recommend using soapstone instead of regular chalk for labeling since it doesn't create any dust and is safe to consume.

Hopeless Hostess Tip

No board, no problem! If you're strapped for cash or looking to do something a little less traditional, you can still serve delicious spreads. Try using antique plates for a more eclectic vibe, or even slap some parchment paper down on your kitchen table! Whichever surface you choose, just make sure you're considering the food you'll be serving, how much space you'll need, and the story you're trying to tell with your food.

THE ACCESSORIES

Aside from the board itself, there are some other items that you'll want to have on hand when you're hosting. Stylish utensils, dippers, and ramekins pull everything together and play a key role in building a jaw-dropping food display. Here are a few of my favorites.

Honey Dipper

Ah, the beloved honey dipper! This one is an absolute must-have and a big hit at every party. If you have honey on your board, opt to serve it neatly and beautifully with a wood or gold-tone stainless steel dipper. A honey dipper not only is an adorable touch to your board but also reduces the waste that comes from spooning gobs of honey onto your plate. The crevices of the dipper keep the honey from accumulating, and if you keep it spinning, the honey won't drip until you're ready to use it. A drizzle is all you need!

Ramekins

Ramekins or tiny bowls are perfect for holding honey, jam, nuts, briny olives and cornichons, and zingy pickled red onions (page 147). They can also add texture and dimension to your spread. Depending on the size of the board and the size of your ramekins, you will likely only need one to three of them. They should be able to hold 2 to 3 ounces. Buy a matching set if you want a uniform, refined look, or purchase mismatched ramekins that fit your needs and board theme. If a guest has a food allergy, ramekins are a great way to separate tricky ingredients from the rest of the board.

Cheese Knives & Other Cheese Tools

When it comes to cheese knives, I can't tell you how many times a party guest has asked me: "What the heck is this for?" Just like a chef uses various knives for different ingredients, there are different knives for different kinds of cheese. The following is by no means a comprehensive list–and I'll discuss cheeses in more detail soon–but here's a quick cheat sheet on how to use some of the most common cheese tools you'll come across.

CHEESE FORK: While not a knife, it's almost always included in any cheese knife set because it has many purposes. The two pointed prongs are great for picking up sliced cheese or other accoutrements, like cornichons, fruits, and vegetables. It also comes in handy when you need to hold a hard cheese in place as you use the chisel knife to slice off a piece.

CHEESE PLANE: With its spatula-like paddle, the cheese plane is used to shave off thin slices of semisoft cheeses, like young Gouda, fontina, and Comté. It's great if you want consistently thin, even pieces to eat or use on top of salads, crostini, etc.

CHISEL KNIFE: Also known as a flat knife, this knife's elongated blade on the top is used to cut aged, semihard cheeses, like Asiago, Gruyère, and provolone. Hold the blade over the top of the cheese and push down.

PARMESAN KNIFE: Imagine having an entire knife dedicated to you—that's how amazing Parmesan is! (I'll go into why it's my favorite cheese ever a little later.) Because of its shape, it's also referred to as a heart knife, pear knife, or spade knife. It features a pointed tip and sharp, long edge for digging into hard cheeses, like Parmesan and Grana Padano.

PLANE KNIFE: Sometimes called a narrow plane knife or trapezium knife, this tool is great for semihard cheeses, like cheddar, Gouda, and Emmentaler. While it's similar to the chisel knife in how it's used, this knife tends to be more rectangular and offers two sharp sides instead of one. Press down on the cheese block with the top of the knife, then slice again using the side for a smaller piece.

PRONGED KNIFE: This knife, also referred to as forked-tipped spear, is very versatile. The blade is thin and has a small surface area, which allows you to slice a softer cheese without it sticking. The prong makes it easy to pick up your piece and transfer it to your plate. Use this knife for soft to semihard cheeses anywhere on the scale, from Camembert to Parmesan.

SPREADER: This one is pretty self-explanatory. Also known as a spatula knife, a spreader has a dull edge and rounded blade, which is perfect for soft, spreadable cheeses, like Gorgonzola or Brie.

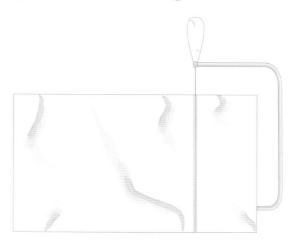

WIRE SLICER: This is an absolute must-have for me! It can be difficult to get a slice of delicate, soft cheese without squishing it from the pressure of the knife, but a wire slicer can save the day. Push down ever so gently to get a clean slice from the softer cheeses, like mozzarella and goat cheese (chèvre).

Various Serving Utensils

Offering your guests a way to easily pick up food without using their hands is always a good (and sanitary) idea. I've found that having a go-to collection of serving utensils takes a lot of the guesswork out of setting up, making it a breeze. These are a few utensils I always keep on hand.

COCKTAIL STICKS/TOOTHPICKS: Stylish charcuterie picks are perfect for just about anything on a board, plus they can double as an eating utensil so guests don't have to eat with their fingers. Simply use disposable wooden toothpicks or find specialty picks that match your theme online or at your favorite home goods retailer.

PETITE SPOONS: These are nice to have for scooping jams and other spreadables. A teaspoon is perfect for smaller ramekins of jam or olive spread, and a tablespoon works well for your larger dips, like hummus, vegetable dip, etc. Using petite spoons with shorter handles makes the board look less cluttered while still being functional.

TONGS: These are great to have for nearly everything on your board. Invest in a set of beautiful, classic walnut tongs for something you can use time and time again. If your board is traveling with you to a party, consider bringing some disposable bamboo tongs. They're environmentally friendly and super cute. Hang them over the side of a mason jar for an organized display.

Hopeless Hostess Tip

While the overall ambiance sets the scene for any event, your accessories can be used to pull the entire look together. I love a uniform look, which lets the beauty of the ingredients shine, but mismatched items—like those vintage spoons your mom has stashed in the basement—can really make a statement! Sourcing items from thrift stores and discount stores like HomeGoods is a great way to start your collection without breaking the bank. But keep in mind that too many competing colors and patterns could leave your board feeling cluttered and chaotic.

THE INGREDIENTS

One of my favorite things about cheese, charcuterie, and snack boards is how creative you can get when deciding what to serve. But it can be overwhelming to know where to start. From prepared foods to seasonal produce to the leftovers that have been sitting around in your fridge, you can make the most of what you have on hand. The following are some of my favorite items to use on boards, but these lists are meant to be guides and thought-starters for you.

Cheese

It's a big cheesy world out there with a lot to consider–different origins, flavors, textures . . . the list goes on. To get you started, here's a crash course in cheese that highlights a few things I think are important to know as a beginner. Everything I've learned about cheese has come from people far more knowledgeable. If you're looking to learn more, I recommend seeking out resources by those with a depth of knowledge in the space.

FRESH
(Burrata, Feta, Cotija, Goat Cheese)

Fresh cheese is essentially cheese in its youngest form, made of cheese curds that haven't been pressed or aged. It's rindless and bright white in color and offers a smooth and creamy texture. It's typically fairly mild in flavor, which makes it great for salads, spreading over toast, mixing into sauces, and more. Make sure to enjoy them within a few days of purchasing.

SOFT-RIPENED
(Brie, Camembert, Fromager d'Affinois, Humboldt Fog)

Soft-ripened cheeses have a "bloomy rind," which adds a level of complexity and texture that makes the flavor special. Repeat after me: You. Can. Eat. The. Rind. Soft-ripened cheeses are often described as having a buttery, mushroomy, and creamy flavor profile. Due to the nature of their soft, creamy interior, you'll typically see them-served in wedges or as a full wheel, with the rind encasing the cheese to provide stability. Enjoy these with any board, on a sandwich, or in your mac 'n' cheese (like my Cracker-Crusted Baked Mac & Brie recipe on page 158).

SEMISOFT
(Fontina, Havarti, Muenster, Jarlsberg)

Semisoft cheese is smooth and creamy. Most of these cheeses have a milder flavor, so they're a great option for picky eaters. Because of their high moisture content, they're great for melting but can be difficult to slice or shred at room temperature.

SEMIHARD
(Cheddar, Swiss, Gouda, Gruyère)

The perfect balance of aridity and moisture is what gives these cheeses their firmer consistency. They are aged anywhere from one to six months, which means a milder flavor than a longer-aged cheese, but the aging process still creates a concentrated rich, buttery flavor. Semihard cheeses are also an excellent option for melting . . . I'm talking an epic grilled cheese like the ones on my fancy grilled-cheese board (page 89).

BLUE-VEINED
(Danish Blue, Gorgonzola, Roquefort)

Blue-veined cheeses are also semisoft, but I think they deserve their own category (and a lot of experts think so too!) because of their deliciously pungent flavor and unique characteristics. The "blue vein" comes from the mold Penicillium, which creates greenish-gray or blue lines throughout the cheese. There are all types of blue cheese: some are made from sheep's or goat's milk, but it is most commonly made using cow's milk.

HARD
(Parmigiano-Reggiano, Pecorino Romano, Manchego)

As you might assume from the name, hard cheese is very firm in texture. This cheese is aged anywhere from six to thirty-six months, which heavily impacts the intensity of the flavor profile. Longer-aged cheeses such as these will have less moisture and begin to form natural crystals, which I like to expertly refer to as flavor bombs, and is my absolute favorite aspect of cheese and why I love Parmigiano-Reggiano so dearly. The rinds, while typically too hard to eat, can impart great flavor and umami to recipes, like soups and sauces.

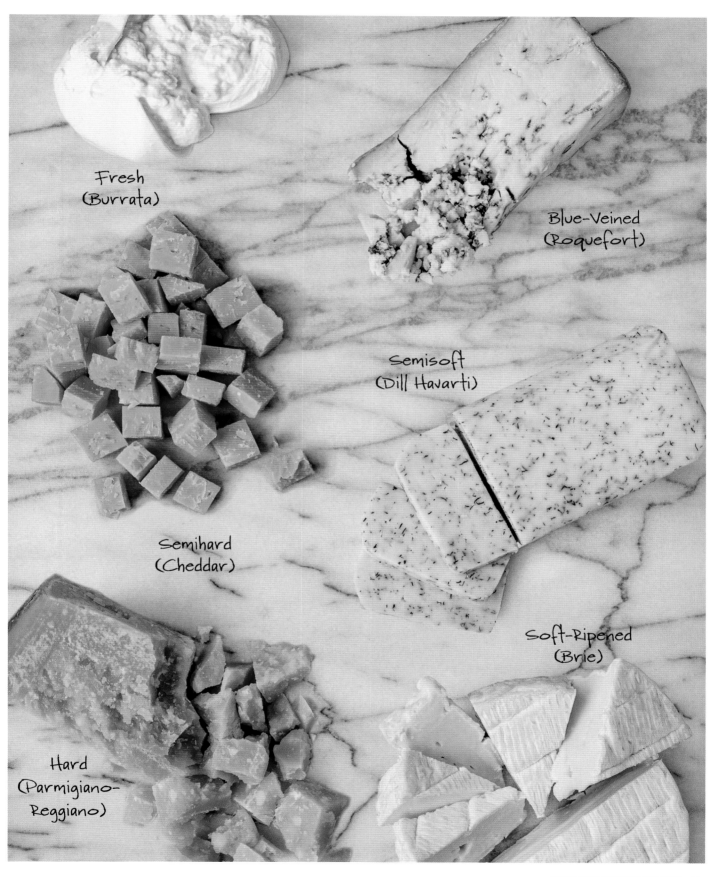

Fresh
(Burrata)

Blue-Veined
(Roquefort)

Semisoft
(Dill Havarti)

Semihard
(Cheddar)

Soft-Ripened
(Brie)

Hard
(Parmigiano-
Reggiano)

Prosciutto

Genoa Salami

Mortadella

Pâté

Chorizo

Bresaola

Fresh Fruits & Veggies

Using fresh in-season produce packs a huge punch! It not only tastes better but also has higher nutritional value, is more environmentally friendly, and is typically more affordable. Plus, the colors are so pretty! You can't go wrong with fresh produce, but a few of my go-tos include grapes, berries of all kinds, citrus, figs, cucumbers, cherry tomatoes, carrots, and radishes. Take a peek at my quick reference guide to seasonal produce on page 14.

Carbs & Crunchy Things

Always offer an assortment of artisanal crackers and fresh bread to accompany your beautiful boards! While crackers are really just vehicles for cheese (in my humble opinion), they can elevate the flavors, textures, and colors of a spread. I use a lot of flavored crackers on my boards because I love the way different seasonings pair with cheese. I like to use herby crackers with fresh cheeses and sweet, fruity ones with earthier aged cheeses, but feel free to use your favorites. I know they can take up a lot of room, so if you want to save space on the board for cheese and charcuterie, opt to make a carb board (page 196) on the side for your crackers and bread.

Crunch from both crackers and things like nuts add a textural element that completes every bite, so be sure to always include some on your board. I'm a big fan of pistachios, almonds, walnuts, the Candied Nuts on page 145, and the Savory Spiced Nuts on page 143.

Charcuterie

Charcuterie (shaar-koo-tuh-ree) is just a fancy way of saying cured meats. The word derives from fifteenth-century France, where instead of letting their leftover meat go to waste, they would cure it to preserve it without refrigeration. Nowadays, in addition to the meat itself, the word *charcuterie* is used loosely to describe a cheese and cured meat board. While this is technically correct (since these boards do have cured meats), it's important to understand the nuances of the word. For example, my Afternoon Pick-Me-Up board (page 82) would be a cheese board, and my S'more, Please! board (page 76) would be a snack board, since neither offer cured meats.

Some of the charcuterie you'll find on these boards include: Genoa salami (cured pork sausage), chorizo (smoky cured sausage), bresaola (air-dried beef), coppa (air-dried pork), prosciutto (dry-cured Italian ham), calabrese (spicy cured salami), soppressata (dry salami), mortadella (original bologna), and pâté (meat paste).

Hopeless Hostess Tip

Produce is at its best when it's grown and harvested in season. In-season produce is widely available and affordable—it also tastes better, which increases the overall appeal of your board. The following reference list will help you select produce on your board, but always remember that item availability is dependent on your region and growing season. Produce availability will vary.

SPRING
Apricots
Artichokes
Asparagus
Avocados
Broccoli rabe
Carrots
Chives
Collards
Mangos
Pineapples
Rhubarb
Snap peas, snow peas
   & pea pods
Strawberries

SUMMER
Bell peppers
Blackberries
Blueberries
Broccoli
Champagne grapes
Cherries
Cucumbers
Gooseberries
Green beans
Mangos
Nectarines
Peaches
Plums
Raspberries
Tomatoes
Watermelon
Zucchini

FALL
Apples
Butternut squash
Carrots
Cauliflower
Cranberries
Edamame
Figs
Gourds
Grapes
Mushrooms
Pears
Pomegranate
Pumpkins
Quince
Sweet potatoes
Swiss chard

WINTER
Chestnuts
Clementines
Grapefruit
Kale
Lemons
Mandarins
Oranges
Radicchio
Radishes
Rutabagas
Tangerines
Turnips
Winter squash

Not everything on your board needs to be from scratch! While I share some recipes throughout the book for homemade items that would work great on your boards, there is no shame in the store-bought game. You'll find a lot of store-bought and prepared ingredients in this book. Why? Because it's easier! The last thing anyone wants is a stressed-out host! If you're pressed for time or just aren't the type to whip up a batch of jam, hummus, chicken salad, or baked goods, add them to your grocery list.

Garnishes & Finishing Touches

You eat with your eyes first, right? If we're going through all this trouble to pick the perfect ingredients, then we better make our finished product Instagram-worthy! (More on this on page 199.)

Garnishes and finishing touches can cover any blank spots on your board, add visual appeal, elaborate on your theme, and ultimately pull the entire spread together. In addition to gorgeous pops of color, fresh herbs and leafy greens can really elevate a bite! Topping a slice of mozzarella with fresh basil is always a winner, and the bitterness of leafy greens can help complement the sweetness of fruits and the richness of cheeses.

Edible flowers are guaranteed to surprise and delight your guests. But it's not only their eye-catching colors and intoxicating fragrance that makes them special—they can also add an unexpected and exciting flavor to your bite! You can typically find these at your local florist or farmers market, but if you're having trouble, you can also find them online (see page 202 for where I purchase mine) and have them shipped right to your door. I love using marigolds, lavender, pansies, chamomile, honeysuckle, daylily, or squash blossoms. Make sure to taste your flowers to ensure that their flavor complements the cheeses on your board, and then place them next to or on their respective pairings to help guide your guests.

You should also consider a few decorative items that might add a little excitement or flare. For example, plan a few days ahead for New Year's Eve and splurge on some edible gold flakes (page 134). Use a fun cookie cutter to shape your soft cheese. Or add googly eyes to make your Halloween board a little spookier (page 95). I've even used a pair of plastic sunglasses on a board before. (Yes, it is as strange as it sounds. Check out my Friends Reunion Special Board on my Instagram to see what I mean!)

Above all, never feel like you *have* to buy specialty items to have a unique board—what makes each one special is the time and effort you put into it! Because of this, I do my best to provide easy alternatives wherever possible.

BUILDING YOUR BOARD

Now that we've talked about what you'll need, let's get to the fun part! Assembling the board is where your creativity gets to shine. The following steps are how I approach building a traditional cheese board, and this section provides the basic reasons behind the where and why.

You'll also want to keep in mind a few ground rules as you develop your artfully designed board. First, think about the occasion you're attending and tailor your board to the event. How many people will be there? How big should your board be?

Next, remember to maintain balance across the board with regard to design and ingredients. If you have a lot of green on one side, try to match that on the other side. Create a balance of cheese, meat, produce, and dips throughout the board so one component doesn't overpower the others.

Last, try your best not to overcrowd or clutter your board. Great boards are made up of hand-selected ingredients that pair well together. I know it's easy to go overboard with so many enticing options to choose from, but try to refrain from making your board look like you've emptied out the entirety of your fridge and pantry.

For some easy ways to elevate your presentation, look at my tips in the Hopeless Hostess Appendix on page 189.

Step 1: Choose your board

A few things to consider when selecting the base for your masterpiece: How many people are you feeding? Are you traveling with your board? Will any of your selections stain? You can choose more than one surface, if needed.

Step 2: Place your ramekins or small bowls

It's easy to forget these once you get going, and you'll want to make sure you save space for dips, honey, jam, briny items, etc. Two per board is typically enough, but you can increase the number if you're using a larger surface area.

Step 5: Add your carbs

A handful of crackers or slices of bread add texture and color variation, but it's best to limit the amount of space you devote to them to save room for other things.

Step 6: Layer your charcuterie

Layer in your charcuterie next. The rule of thumb is 2 ounces of meat per person for an appetizer and more for a meal. Two to three different kinds of meat provide a nice assortment for your guests to choose from.

Step 3: Add your cheeses

This helps make sure that you reserve the prime real estate for the good stuff! Add your styled cheese, making sure any hard cheeses are sliced for easy grabbing. A rule of thumb is to serve 3 ounces of cheese per person for an appetizer and more for a meal.

Step 4: Place larger produce

These foods will be tough to squeeze in later, so it's good to get them on the board early. They create a base layer to build upon when you add some of the filler items in step 7.

Step 7: Fill in the gaps

The final touches! Fill any open spaces with smaller produce, nuts, and other garnishes or bits.

Hopeless Hostess Tip

Before you get to building your board, take a moment to think about your vision. Your spread can reflect the flavors, textures, and pairings that you love, or you can allow yourself to become inspired by your favorite holiday, color combination, television show, or cuisine to create something special. Are you celebrating a birthday? Think about some of the guest of honor's favorite foods. Hosting your annual Independence Day party? Brainstorm something red, white, and blue, like my Fourth of July board on page 75. Having a viewing party for *The Bachelor*? Include fresh roses or shoot your shot at making the beloved salami rose (page 194). Whatever the occasion, consider the experience you're trying to create for your guests and let your board bring that to life. Don't be afraid to step out of your comfort zone!

USING
THIS BOOK

··

We're almost there! Now that we're inching closer to getting our hands dirty, let's take a moment to explore how you can make this book work for you. Think of it as peeking behind the curtain of my brain to understand why I've labeled, categorized, and organized the book the way that I have.

THE BOARDS

As I've mentioned before, these boards are meant to be a guide to creating your own perfect version, and I've given you some basic information to help get you started, like measurements, difficulty level, expected investment, dietary labels, and more. I think these are some of the most important factors to consider when building a board. With this information readily available before you start, you'll be able to easily identify which boards are going to work for your event, schedule, and wallet!

Ingredient Amounts

Each board in this book includes approximate ingredient amounts to give an idea of how much to purchase or whether you happen to have enough on hand already, but your dream spread will depend on your specific creative vision and practical needs. The size and shape of your board, how many people you're feeding, and your food preferences all affect how much of something you'll wind up using. However, a good baseline is 3 ounces of cheese per person and 2 ounces of meat per person. Really, you can't go wrong, so don't stress too much about the snacks!

Seasonality

The changing of seasons, celebrating holidays, and gathering for events drives inspiration and sparks creativity when it comes to hosting, so I organized the boards by season: spring, summer, fall, and winter. The memories and feelings we're able to cultivate through food are so powerful, and I love that each and every season offers different ways to bring us around the table to share laughs, stories, and most important, delicious food.

Some boards are related to my own experiences, and some are aligned to holidays or events, like the Oktoberfest board on page 102. Others are more universal and instead highlight seasonal ingredients (which can be repurposed throughout the year with a few simple substitutions), like the Summertime Citrus, Mozzarella & Prosciutto board on page 63.

Keep in mind that the seasonality of some ingredients could affect their availability. For example, some of the Christmas-themed boards use spiced cheeses or sweets that are only available in the wintertime. But if you can't find a specific ingredient, use your best judgment and personal preference to select a substitution that will pair well with the other elements on the board.

Allergens & Other Dietary Needs

Each board is labeled with the following icons so you can easily find spreads that fit your needs. For quick-reference lists of meat-free boards, easy weeknight meals, and other culinary considerations, turn to page 187.

- **VEGAN**
- **VEGETARIAN**
- **GLUTEN-FREE**

Investment

One huge factor when creating a board is your budget. If you've ever made a snack board before, you know firsthand how quickly those items can add up! For this reason, I call out the approximate investment for each board. However, if you see a board that you'd like to make that is out of your price range, don't sweat it! You can always substitute some of the pricier items for extra veggies, fruits, snack mixes, etc. Please be aware that these are just estimates and the actual amounts will vary, depending on where you live and where you shop. For my favorite wallet-friendly snack boards, turn to page 187.

- $$$ **UP TO $40**
- $$$ **BETWEEN $41 AND $85**
- $$$ **ABOVE $85**

Difficulty

Each board in this book has been assigned a difficulty rating–not to entice or discourage you from making one board over another but to mentally prepare you for the time and effort required. Some days we have more time than others to expertly fold salami! These indicators help you understand how involved a board might be so you can choose accordingly. For a handy list of boards that can be made in under 20 minutes, check out page 187.

●○○ **EASY:** These boards should take you 30 minutes or less. They use mostly store-bought prepared ingredients and require little to no home cooking. The techniques used are fairly simple and won't require much practice to master. If you're totally new to snack boards, give Bountiful Berries (page 31) a try.

●●○ **INTERMEDIATE:** Like the Ultimate Taco Tuesday board on page 67, these should take around 45 minutes. They use some store-bought prepared ingredients, but you'll also have to do some cooking. The techniques aren't difficult or cumbersome, but they might require you to spend some time practicing your folding or slicing before plating.

●●● **DIFFICULT:** Don't shy away from the more difficult boards! While they may take you an hour or more to assemble, they are absolute show-stoppers. (Feast your eyes on the Ooey-Gooey Fondue-y board on page 86.) They might use a few prepared ingredients, but they require you to spend more time in the kitchen whipping up components. The techniques are a little more sophisticated, which will take more time to master. These boards may also include items that require you to purchase them online in advance, like the witch's cauldron on the Halloween-themed Toil & Treats (page 95).

THE RECIPES

I've included a handful of my favorite recipes throughout the book. Some of them are included within the boards themselves, like the Brie Brûlée on the Fall Harvest board (page 85), and others are stand-alone recipes gathered in chapter 6, like the snack-board staples Candied Nuts (page 145) and Creamy Hummus (page 140). Feel free to pick and choose how you incorporate them into your boards, if you do at all. For example, if you think the Elote Dip (page 141) would work well on the Ultimate Taco Tuesday board (page 67), add it to the list!

THE EXTRAS

If you picked up this book to learn how to assemble fun and fancy snack boards, you're in the right place! But there's so much more in here for you, too. These pages are packed full of ideas on how to elevate your next soiree beyond your board.

I share my super fun cocktail recipes (the Autumn Harvest Punch below is on page 174), favorite flavor combinations (so you can impress your friends!), and tips and tricks for styling your food. There's even a Hopeless Hostess Appendix (page 185) that covers everything you need to know about prepping, styling, and more!

Ultimately, my goal in sharing all this information is to leave you in the most capable hands . . . your own! Through these boards, recipes, tips, and tricks, I want you to feel empowered to harness your passion and create something beautiful. Although this book is filled with ways to use a special event or holiday to inspire you, remember that a board can come together on a whim and without a theme, expensive ingredients, or elaborate decor. This is your reminder to allow the small things to fill your cup—or should I say board? Be creative, be adventurous (and yes, that means you should try the blue cheese), and most important, be proud of the edible piece of art you've created.

2
SPRING

CLASSY CRUDITÉ

●●● $$$

Crudité, which actually just means "raw things," is a beautiful addition to any party. Full of bright, crisp colors and raw ingredients, this board is an elegant upgrade of your classic veggie tray. *Serves 6 to 8*

Accessories: 2 ramekins

Board: 14-by-10-inch rectangle, wood

5 miniature cucumbers

1 bunch tri-color carrots

5 radishes, tops removed and set aside

10 to 12 sugar snap peas

¼ head purple cauliflower

6 to 8 broccolini stalks

1 bunch asparagus

1 bunch celery

10 tri-color cherry tomatoes

1 cup Creamy Hummus (page 140) or store-bought

1 cup Creamy Veggie Dip (page 138) or store-bought

Mint sprigs

Edible Flowers

1 handful Crispy Chickpeas (page 144) or store-bought

1. Using a sharp knife, thinly slice the cucumbers, carrots, and radishes. To achieve this look, I used smaller vegetables to get short, thin pieces. Open the pea pods and cut the broccoli into smaller florets. Trim and separate the broccolini, asparagus, and celery. Halve the tomatoes or keep them whole.

2. Place two small bowls or ramekins to the board. Fill them with the hummus and veggie dip.

3. Begin to layer the vegetables, in no particular order, starting from the outside of the board and working inward toward the ramekins. Be sure to keep in mind the variation between colors, sizes, and shapes as you arrange the vegetables.

4. Garnish your board with the reserved radish tops, mint sprigs, and edible flowers. Top the hummus with the chickpeas.

My Perfect Bite: Broccolini with a large scoop of hummus and crispy chickpeas.

Bottoms Up! A fragrant, citrus-led sauvignon blanc.

While English peas are best to achieve a plentiful, open-shelled look, sugar snap peas work just as well, and their pods are edible, unlike English peas. Shelling the peas is easy: Pinch the flower end of the pod and pull the string down toward the other end to remove it. Separate the two sides of the pod and place it on the board.

BOUNTIFUL BERRIES

Brighten your mood and welcome the flavors of spring with this sweet and super easy berry board. Stick with my suggestions or go for whatever is in season, but pile it high with all the berries you can get your hands on.
Serves 4 to 6

Accessories: 1 small bowl or ramekin

Board: 13-by-8-inch rectangle, wood

½ (8-ounce) container cream cheese fruit dip

3 blackberries, halved, plus a few handfuls left whole

Mint sprigs

1 (7-ounce) block blueberry cobbler cheddar, sliced

1 (5-ounce) log honey goat cheese

8 lemon shortbread cookies

2 handfuls strawberries

2 handfuls golden berries, golden raspberries, or cherries

2 handfuls raspberries

1 handful blueberries

Edible flowers

1. Place a small bowl or ramekin on the board. Fill it with the fruit dip and garnish with the halved blackberries and mint sprigs.

2. Layer the slices of cheddar, placing one on top of the other, around the ramekin of fruit dip. Place the goat cheese on the board and slightly crumble one side using a butter knife.

3. Lay the cookies on the board, placing them around the edges. Fill in the remainder of the board with the remaining blackberries, the strawberries, golden berries, raspberries, and blueberries. I recommend starting with the larger berries first and placing the smaller berries on top. Be sure to pay attention to the variation of the colors.

4. Garnish your board with edible flowers.

My Perfect Bite: Lemon shortbread cookie, schmear of honey goat cheese, blackberries, and a sprig of mint.

Bottoms Up! The tart, dry flavors of a dry rosé perfectly complement the sweetness of the berries.

I found blueberry cobbler cheddar at my local grocery store, but any fruity, sweet cheese will work well here.

BUILD-YOUR-OWN BLOODY MARY

●●○ $$$

Let your guests have all the fun with this deconstructed Bloody Mary board! They can make skewers of their favorite fixings or add them directly to the glass. Once everyone is done building their drinks, snack on the leftovers and try pairing different items with cheese! Sprinkling the habanero salt over a cracker with Danish blue cheese gives it a great pop of flavor. *Serves 8*

Accessories: 6 ramekins, wooden skewers or cocktail picks (optional)

Board: 10-by-11-inch rectangle, wood

The Best Bloody Mary Mix

48 ounces tomato juice

6 to 8 ounces vodka of choice

3 tablespoons hot horseradish

3 tablespoons Worcestershire sauce

3 ounces pickle juice

2 teaspoons celery salt

2 teaspoons garlic salt

Pinch freshly ground black pepper

Tabasco sauce

For the Board

1 (7-ounce jar) cornichons

1 (6-ounce) jar Manzanilla olives

½ (16-ounce) jar cocktail onions

½ (12-ounce) jar pepperoncini

6 to 8 cooked jumbo shrimp

Habanero salt or other flavored salt

1 (5-ounce) wedge Danish blue cheese or other blue cheese

1 (8-ounce) block habanero cheddar, sliced

6 to 8 celery stalks

About 15 mini toasts

10 crispy bacon slices

3 lemons, cut into wedges

3 limes, cut into wedges

1 handful cherry tomatoes, halved

2 handfuls pistachios

Dill sprigs

Make a virgin Bloody mix so that guests can add their own alcohol. This way, everyone can create their version of the best Bloody Mary, even if that's a Bloody Maria (tequila) or a virgin Bloody!

I like to cut the block of cheddar into five (1-inch) blocks, flip it on its side, then slice into long, thin pieces, which shows the natural variation within the cheese and creates a cleaner look.

continued »

1. **Make the Bloody Mary Mix:** In a large pitcher, combine the tomato juice, vodka, horseradish, Worcestershire sauce, pickle juice, celery salt, garlic salt, and pepper. Add Tabasco sauce to taste and stir until well combined. Chill in the fridge until your guests arrive.

2. **Assemble the board:** Place six ramekins on the board. For consistency, try to keep five out of six the same size, as they will be holding the toppings for the cocktails. Fill the ramekins with the cornichons, olives, cocktail onions, pepperoncini, shrimp, and habanero salt.

3. Place the blue cheese on the board. Crumble the corner of the blue cheese using a butter knife. Place the cheddar slices on the board.

4. Add the celery, mini toasts, and bacon on the board, followed by the lemons, limes, and tomatoes. Fill in any gaps with the pistachios and garnish with dill sprigs.

5. **Make the drinks:** Moisten the rim of the glass with a lemon or lime wedge. Place some habanero salt on a plate and dip the rim until it's evenly coated. Fill the glasses with ice and top with Bloody Mary mix.

My Perfect Bite: Mini toast, a shmear of blue cheese, and a pepperoncini.

Bottoms Up! Here's what I would have in my Bloody Mary: a habanero salt rim, a celery stalk, jumbo shrimp, pepperoncini, cocktail onion, and two Manzanilla olives.

TASTE OF THE MEDITERRANEAN

Mezze—which means "to taste or snack" in Arabic—is an appetizer made up of a variety of small plates. This mezze board, full of delicious Mediterranean flavors and vibrant colors, has something for everyone! You can make this board even easier with a store-bought feta salad. *Serves 6*

Board: 15-by-11-inch rectangle, wood with rim

Marinated Feta & Olive Salad

½ (8-ounce) block feta, cubed

½ (7-ounce) packaged pitted mixed olives

1 to 2 roasted red peppers

½ lemon, zested and juiced

1 garlic clove, minced

3 tablespoons extra-virgin olive oil

½ teaspoon chopped fresh parsley

½ teaspoon red pepper flakes

½ teaspoon dried oregano

Salt

Freshly ground black pepper

For the Board

1 cup Creamy Hummus (page 140) or store-bought

Extra-virgin olive oil

3 to 4 pita rounds, quartered

8 dolma (stuffed grape leaves)

5 ounces tabbouleh salad

3 marinated artichokes, halved

1 cucumber, sliced

1 to 2 handfuls cherry tomatoes, halved

5 radishes, halved

1 lemon, sliced

Mint sprigs

I usually opt for a small bowl to hold dips, but I love the organic, unpolished look of adding the hummus directly to the board. Since all the flavors blend so beautifully together, having your ingredients touch is perfectly fine! For some other ideas on how to dress up your dips, see page 195.

continued »

1. **Make the Marinated Feta & Olive Salad:** Put the feta, olives, red peppers, lemon zest and juice, garlic, olive oil, parsley, red pepper flakes, and oregano in a medium bowl and mix well to combine. Season with salt and pepper to taste. Allow salad to marinate at least 20 minutes before serving.

2. **Assemble the board:** Place the hummus directly on the board. To get the iconic hummus swirl, in one smooth motion, with the tip of the spoon in the center of the hummus, push the spoon and rotate in a circular pattern. Fill the valley with olive oil.

3. Place the pita pieces on two opposite corners of the board. Place the dolma, tabbouleh salad, and marinated feta and olive salad around the hummus.

4. In the remaining space, add the marinated artichokes, cucumber, tomatoes, radishes, and lemon. Garnish the board with mint sprigs.

My Perfect Bite: A soft piece of pita, a big scoop of creamy hummus, topped with cucumber and feta and olive salad.

Bottoms Up! Crack open a nice bottle of light-bodied, silky pinot noir.

BRIMFUL BRUNCH BOARD

●●○ $$$

Whether you're hosting an elegant brunch for Mother's Day, a bridal shower, or just Sunday Funday with your girlfriends, you can whip this board together with minimum effort. Everything used here requires little to no prep! Gone are the days of slaving over the stove first thing in the morning. This simple-yet-striking board will fill you up and leave you wanting more—more mimosas, that is.
Serves 4 to 6

Accessories: 1 ramekin, 1 small plate, wax paper

Board: 16-inch round, wood with handles

4 to 6 large eggs

¼ cup orange blossom honey or other honey

4 to 6 pieces cinnamon coffee cake

1 stick salted butter

8 Belgian waffles

4 to 6 crispy bacon slices or Candied
  Bacon (page 143)

12 pieces cooked breakfast sausage

1 to 2 handfuls cherries

10 to 15 strawberries

1 to 2 handfuls raspberries

1 to 2 handfuls blueberries

1 to 2 handfuls blackberries

Mint sprigs

Maple syrup, for serving

1. Add 3 inches of water to a pot large enough to hold all your eggs with some space in between them. Cover and bring to a boil over high heat. Carefully add the eggs to the pot straight from the refrigerator. Cover and boil for about 6 minutes, which will give you a jammy center, or 9 minutes for a firmer yolk. (I boil mine for 6 minutes.) While the eggs are cooking, prepare an ice bath. Transfer the eggs to the ice bath and let them sit until you're ready to peel them—or let your guests do the peeling.

2. Fill a ramekin with the honey, place the coffee cake on a small plate, and place the butter on wax paper or another small plate. Arrange them on the board.

3. Add the waffles, placing one on top of the other across the board. Tuck the bacon and breakfast sausage around the waffles.

4. Fill in the remainder of the board with the cherries, raspberries, blueberries, blackberries, and soft-boiled eggs. Garnish with mint sprigs. Serve with the maple syrup on the side.

My Perfect Bite: A fluffy Belgian waffle, covered in melted butter and maple syrup, topped with fresh berries. Breakfast sausage on the side!

Bottoms Up! Mimosa, please! Or two . . . or three . . .

For some added texture, crumple the wax paper a bit!
Perfectly crisp wax paper, who? We aren't trying that hard.

To keep your warm ingredients warm, prepare them according to the package instructions, then arrange them on a rimmed baking sheet, cover them with aluminum foil, and place them in a 200°F oven until you're ready to add them to your board.

C'EST CHARCUTERIE

● ○ ○ $$$

I wanted to give a nod to the traditional charcuterie board inspired by my trips to Paris (*chef's kiss*). This one is primarily composed of an assortment of cured meats and pâté, but I paired them with traditional accoutrements and Roquefort, a world-renowned blue-veined cheese from Southern France. *Serves 5 to 6*

Accessories: 1 small plate

Board: 13-by-18-inch rectangle, wood

1 (4-ounce) wedge Roquefort

½ (5-ounce) package pâté de campagne

2 bunches champagne grapes or regular grapes

¼ loaf French bread, sliced

2 handfuls seeded crackers

3 ounces prosciutto slices, folded

3 ounces bresaola slices, folded

3 ounces soppressata slices, folded

6 cornichons

¼ cup whole-grain mustard

1 to 2 tablespoons fig spread

Rosemary sprigs

1. Place the Roquefort and the pâté on opposite sides of the board. Add the grapes and French bread to the board, placing them around the edges. Place the seeded crackers on small plate off to the side.

2. Fold the prosciutto, bresaola, and soppressata and place them on the board.

3. Add the cornichons, mustard, and a schmear of fig spread. Garnish the board with rosemary sprigs.

My Perfect Bite: A generous spread of Roquefort on a slice of French bread topped with bresaola, fig spread, and a few grapes.

Bottoms Up! Wine at lunchtime? C'est la vie! Pair this with a glass of Syrah, also known as Shiraz.

Pâté (French for "paste") is often associated with wealth and extravagance. If you're new to pâté, give pâté de campagne a try. It's traditionally made with coarse ground pork meat and duck liver with garlic, parsley, onion, and rosemary, making it a savory and easy intro to the delicacy.

TOWERING TEA PARTY

●●● $$$

Grab your girls for a spot of tea, and sip and snack the afternoon away. I opted for an adorable, tiered platter, but don't worry if you don't have something similar. You can serve these items on separate plates for a more linear spread. *Serves 4 to 6*

Board: 3-tiered stand

English Tea Sandwiches

6 slices sandwich bread

4 tablespoons prepared egg salad

4 tablespoons prepared cranberry chicken salad

3 tablespoons cream cheese, softened

¼ English cucumber, thinly sliced

Squeeze of lemon juice

Salt

Freshly ground black pepper

Chives, chopped (optional)

Smoked Salmon & Cream Cheese Bites

6 mini toasts

¼ (4-ounce) package cream cheese, softened

½ (4-ounce) package smoked salmon

Squeeze of lemon juice

¼ cup Quick Pickled Red Onions (page 147) or store-bought

Thyme sprigs (optional)

For the Board

4 scones of choice

5 to 6 bunches champagne or regular grapes

3 fresh figs

8 macarons

1 (8-ounce) round double crème Brie

2 to 3 handfuls mixed berries

Edible flowers

Rosemary sprigs

1. **Make the English Tea Sandwiches:** Cut each slice of bread into two equal pieces, removing the crust. Make two egg salad sandwiches. Make two chicken salad sandwiches. For the cucumber and cream cheese sandwiches, spread cream cheese on one slice of bread and top with cucumber slices. Add a squeeze of lemon and season with salt and pepper. Top with fresh chives, if using, before capping with another piece of bread.

2. **Make the Smoked Salmon & Cream Cheese Bites:** Spread the cream cheese onto the mini toasts. Add a piece smoked salmon and a squeeze of lemon juice. Add pickled red onions, and garnish with fresh thyme, if desired.

3. **Assemble the board:** Starting at the bottom of your serving tower, place the chocolate chip scones, a few bunches of grapes, and some of the fresh figs. On the second tier, place the tea sandwiches, smoked salmon cream cheese bites, and more grapes. On the top tier, place the macarons and the remaining grapes.

4. Slice the Brie into small wedges and place on a small plate. Top with the berries. Garnish the tower with edible flowers and rosemary sprigs.

My Perfect Bite: Each item is made to enjoy individually. I'd reach for a sweet macaron and a small bunch of champagne grapes!

Bottoms Up! Enjoy this spread with a cup of English Earl Grey tea with a dash of milk and pinch of sugar.

I use my favorite store-bought egg and chicken salads to make my mini tea sandwiches, but some other ideas are: crab salad, Bresaola and marinated artichokes, or blue cheese and grapes. The options are endless!

A BOARD
BUILT FOR TWO

● ○ ○ $$$

This scaled-down board is built for two (or one) and is the perfect answer to "What's for dinner?" after a long day at work. With savory and sweet all in one spread, there's no need to plan for multiple courses. Also, you can expect *way* fewer dishes to wash once you're done.
Serves 2

Accessories: 1 ramekin

Board: 10-inch round, wood

¼ cup apricot or other fruit spread

Mint sprigs

1 (4-ounce) package Bijou (aged goat cheese)

1 (3-ounce) wedge blue Stilton

1 (2-ounce) wedge Manchego, sliced

6 ounces prosciutto slices, folded

1 bunch grapes, any color

½ kiwi

1 handful blackberries

1 handful blueberries

1 handful seeded crackers

1 to 2 handfuls sesame-honey cashews

1 to 2 handfuls dark chocolate-covered pretzels

Rosemary sprigs (optional)

Edible flowers (optional)

1. Place a ramekin on the board. Fill with the apricot spread and garnish with a mint sprig.

2. Add the goat cheese, Stilton, and Manchego slices to the board. Crumble the corner of the Stilton with a butter knife.

3. Build a prosciutto ribbon by placing folded prosciutto, one after the other, and connecting each slice to the next. For step-by-step directions, see page 193.

4. Add the grapes, kiwi, crackers, pretzels, blueberries, and blackberries. Fill in the remaining space with the cashews. Garnish with rosemary and flowers, if using.

My Perfect Bite: Schmear of goat cheese and apricot spread on top of a dark chocolate-covered pretzel.

Bottoms Up! A big ol' glass of Malbec! You know the glass I mean—the one that fits the entire bottle.

SAY "CHEEZ"

●○○ $$$

This plant-based board is perfect for a gathering with friends that have dietary restrictions. It's super versatile—for example, you can easily make this gluten-free by using gluten-free crackers or more substantial by adding plant-based pepperoni or other faux meats. This board might lack dairy and meat products, but it certainly does not lack flavor!
Serves 6

Accessories: 1 small bowl

Board: 12-inch square, wood

1 bunch dandelion greens or other leafy greens

½ cup Creamy Hummus (page 140) or store-bought

2 fresh figs, halved

½ cup walnut pieces

1 (6.5-ounce) cashew cream chive wheel

1 (7-ounce) block plant-based mature cheddar, sliced

1 (5-ounce) wedge plant-based Parmesan, cut into chunks

2 bunches grapes, any color

1 to 2 handfuls seeded crackers

1 cucumber, sliced

3 radishes, sliced

3 heirloom tomatoes or other large tomatoes, quartered

1 to 2 handfuls blueberries

1 broccolini stalk, separated into sprigs

1. Place the greens on the board. They should act like a bed for the other ingredients and cover the whole board. Leave some hanging over the edges of the board to create a look of abundance.

2. Fill a small bowl with the hummus. Garnish with some of the sliced fig and walnuts.

3. Place cashew cream wheel, cheddar, and Parmesan on opposite sides of the board. Place the grapes, crackers, and cucumber on the board around the cheeses.

4. Fill in the open space with the radishes, tomatoes, blueberries, and the remaining figs and walnuts. Garnish with broccolini sprigs.

My Perfect Bite: A wedge of cashew cream chive cheese, with grapes and a walnut on top.

Bottoms Up! The vibrant acidity and savory qualities from a chardonnay would pair perfectly with the cashew cream.

Today, there are so many options for those following a plant-based diet to get their cheese fix—some of my favorite brands are Miyoko's and Violife. You can find them at most large grocery stores, including Whole Foods and Target, or online.

I bought my pot o' gold online for next to nothing! Plus, it can also be repurposed as a witch's cauldron on your Halloween board (page 95).

LUCK O' THE IRISH

●●○ $$$

Or should I say *potluck* of the Irish? Either way, this Irish-inspired board features many treasures that are sure to please even the littlest leprechaun. My favorite part? The gleaming pot of gold at the end of your pastrami rainbow! I even used a clover-shaped cookie cutter for a fun twist on a standard Brie wheel. *Serves 6 to 8*

Accessories: 1 ramekin, 1 small bowl or pot for gold

Board: 13-inch round, wood

¼ cup whole-grain mustard

1 bag milk chocolate gold coins

1 (5-ounce) wedge Irish cheddar with red wine or plain Irish cheddar

1 (7-ounce) wedge Irish Gouda, cubed

1 (8-ounce) round double crème Brie

1 pound thinly sliced pastrami, folded

2 handfuls seeded crackers

2 handfuls white chocolate pretzels

1 bunch green grapes

1 to 2 green apples, diced

10 to 15 green olives

1 (6-ounce) package blackberries

Rosemary sprigs

1. Place a ramekin and a bowl for your gold on the board. Fill the ramekin with the mustard and the bowl with gold coins. Add some additional gold coins around the bowl to make it look like it is overflowing.

2. Place the cheddar, Gouda, and Brie on the board.

3. Starting on one end of the board, begin to fold and place the pastrami in a ribbonlike fashion. Continue throughout the entire board and finish on the other side, creating a long train of pastrami.

4. Add the crackers, pretzels, grapes, apples, olives, and blackberries to the board. Garnish the board with rosemary sprigs.

My Perfect Bite: Seeded cracker, piece of Irish cheddar with red wine, pastrami, and a little swipe of whole-grain mustard.

Bottoms Up! No doubt, you need an Irish stout! Sláinte!

EASTER SUNDAY BOARD

●●○　　　$$$

Elevate your Easter basket with a festive spring charcuterie board to snack on before your main course. I played off an Easter Bunny theme with Bunny Bait trail mix, marshmallow bunnies, and a bowl of edible grass topped with chocolate Easter eggs. It's as much fun for the kids as it is for the parents! *Serves 8 to 10*

Accessories: 1 ramekin, 2 medium bowls, 1 bunny-shaped Easter egg or plastic Easter egg (optional)

Board: 16-inch round, wood with handles

½ (5-ounce) package honeycomb

1 (5-ounce) round Caramelized Onion & Herbs Boursin or other cheese spread

1 (1-ounce) package edible grass or microgreens

1 handful candy-coated chocolate eggs

2 handfuls Bunny Bait Trail Mix or other sweet trail mix

1 (8-ounce) round double crème Brie

1 (6-ounce) wedge Wensleydale (fresh sheep's or cow's milk cheese) with apricots or other fruit-studded cheese

5 marshmallow bunnies

3 bunches muscat grapes

½ English cucumber, sliced

6 ounces prosciutto slices, folded

2 to 3 handfuls sourdough flatbread bites

1 to 2 handfuls dried apricots

1 to 2 handfuls blueberries

3 chocolate-dipped kiwi slices

2 chocolate-dipped pineapple slices

Fresh thyme sprigs

Edible flowers

1. Place the ramekin, bowls, and the Easter egg, if using, on the board.

2. Fill the ramekin with honeycomb. Fill one bowl with Boursin and the other with edible grass and chocolate eggs. Add the trail mix to the Easter egg.

3. If desired, cut out two butterfly-shaped pieces from the Brie using a cookie cutter. Place the Brie and Wensleydale on opposite sides of the board.

4. Add the marshmallow bunnies, grapes, and cucumber slices. Build a prosciutto ribbon by placing folded prosciutto, one after the other, and connecting each slice to the next. For step-by-step directions, see page 193.

5. Fill in any open space with the flatbread bites, apricots, blueberries, chocolate-covered fruit, and cashews. Garnish with thyme sprigs and edible flowers.

My Perfect Bite: Crumbled Wensleydale with apricots over a cracker with a slice of prosciutto and a spoonful of honeycomb.

Bottoms Up! Celebrate the spring season with a Vanilla Old-Fashioned (page 172)! The sweet yet bitter cocktail pairs perfectly with the board's bright flavors.

Fancy up your fruit by dunking it into melted chocolate! It's simple and adds a super sweet touch to any board. All you need is a package of semisweet or milk chocolate morsels and a tablespoon of coconut oil. Combine and microwave until melted, stirring about every 30 seconds. Dip your fruit into the chocolate and place on parchment paper until it hardens. Store in the fridge until you're ready to serve.

I love dragon fruit because it looks like something straight out of a Dr. Seuss book. It's bright pink on the outside and has fun polka dots inside. You can also find pink-fleshed fruit that is much brighter and sweeter. You can usually find them at Whole Foods or online, but if you can't, replace it with kiwi or sliced pears.

SPRING FLORAL

●●● $$$

Swing into spring with this elegant floral board! Full of blooming flowers and bright colors, this board is as welcoming as the warming weather. It's also the perfect way to show Mom you love her on Mother's Day. For detailed instructions on how to give your cheeses flower power, see page 191. *Serves 6*

Accessories: 1 ramekin, 1 small bowl

Board: 15-inch round, wood with rim

¼ cup wildflower honey

½ (8-ounce) package quark cheese (whipped cow's milk)

Edible Flowers

1 (8-ounce) round triple crème Brie

1 (4-ounce) log truffle goat cheese

12 to 15 herbed flatbread crackers

4 ounces prosciutto slices, folded

2 ounces soppressata slices

3 bunches green grapes

1 dragon fruit, sliced

1 to 2 handfuls raspberries

1 to 2 handfuls blackberries

1 to 2 handfuls blueberries

1 green apple, sliced

1 to 2 handfuls truffle Marcona almonds

1. Place a ramekin and a small bowl on the board. Fill the ramekin with the honey and the bowl with the quark. Garnish with flowers.

2. Place the flower-covered Brie and goat cheese on the board. For step-by-step directions for making floral cheese, see page 191.

3. Add the crackers, prosciutto, soppressata, grapes, and dragon fruit slices. For step-by-step directions for making a sopressata rose, see page 194.

4. Fill the remaining space with the raspberries, blackberries, blueberries, apple slices, and almonds. Garnish with more flowers.

My Perfect Bite: Herbed cracker, green apple slice, dollop of truffle goat cheese, and a drizzle of honey.

Bottoms Up! This board pairs perfectly with the fruity and floral aromas of a tall glass of prosecco! A toast to you, Mom!

3
SUMMER

MELON BALL SALAD PLATTER

●●○ $$$

This self-serve salad platter is perfect as a summer appetizer or lunch when it's just too hot to cook. I like to serve this with a lemon and shallot vinaigrette, but a balsamic vinaigrette or a squeeze of fresh lemon juice and a drizzle of EVOO would be delicious, too. Feel free to add additional vegetables to make it more substantial and enjoy all that summer produce has to offer! *Serves 4*

Accessories: 1 small cruet or dressing pourer

Board: 15-by-12-inch platter, porcelain

1 (5-ounce) container arugula

1 (8-ounce) package small mozzarella balls

¼ watermelon, scooped into 1-tablespoon balls

¼ cantaloupe, scooped into 1-tablespoon balls

¼ honeydew, scooped into 1-tablespoon balls

4 ounces prosciutto slices

4 ounces Genoa salami slices

¼ cup Candied Nuts (page 145)
    or store-bought, chopped

Mint sprigs

Vinaigrette of choice, for serving

1. Lay down a bed of arugula to cover the entire platter. Add the mozzarella and watermelon, cantaloupe, and honeydew balls to the platter.

2. Fold the prosciutto slices and place them in small pockets across the platter. Fold the salami into tiny roses. For step-by-step directions see page 194. Place them sporadically across the platter.

3. Sprinkle the pecans on top of the other ingredients. Garnish with mint sprigs. Serve with vinaigrette on the side.

My Perfect Bite: A little bit of everything! Choose your favorite melon ball and make sure to grab some fresh arugula and a sliver of prosciutto.

Bottoms Up! This salad platter would pair perfectly with a refreshing Pretty Pink Lemonade Spritzer (page 170)!

Nothing grinds my gears more than realizing I've picked out an unripe melon. To make sure you're not serving lackluster fruit, keep these tips in mind. **Cantaloupe** should have golden undertones (not green) and a subtly sweet, pleasant aroma. **Honeydew** should have a creamy yellow (not green) color and a smooth and waxy rind. The bottom should feel slightly soft when pressed. **Watermelon** should have a rind that's a bit dull, with a yellow field spot, which means it's been ripening on the vine for a long time. You can also give it a couple of knocks. A hollow sound is an indication that it's ripe.

Make sure to look for red, yellow, green, and orange tomatoes. The contrasting colors make for a beyond-beautiful display.

BURRATA & HEIRLOOM TOMATO SALAD

●○○ $$$

Sweet, rich, and creamy burrata paired with the undeniable perfection of in-season heirloom tomatoes is a combination you will never forget. This board is a foolproof addition to your summer soiree. *Serves 6 to 8*

Accessories: 1 ramekin

Board: 13-inch round, wood

5 heirloom tomatoes, cut into ¼-inch-thick slices

1 (8-ounce) package burrata

10 to 20 cherry tomatoes

¼ cup Basil Pesto (page 138) or store-bought

Freshly ground black pepper

Flaky sea salt

Basil leaves

Mint leaves

1. Layer the tomatoes slices on the board. Be sure to pay attention to the color variations to create a vibrant color scheme.

2. Place the burrata on the board. If you have multiple balls, place them on opposite sides of the board. If you have one large ball, place it in right in the center.

3. Add the cherry tomatoes sporadically across the board. You can cut some in half and leave others whole for more textural variety.

4. Drizzle the pesto over the board and top with pepper and salt. Garnish with basil and mint. Serve the remaining pesto on the side in the ramekin.

My Perfect Bite: Green tomato, a heaping spoonful of burrata, and a dollop of basil pesto.

Bottoms Up! Serve this board with a delightfully refreshing yet zesty pinot grigio.

FUN IN THE SUN

See you at the beach! This board is quick to pack and simple to assemble while you're sitting in the sand. Pro tip: Watch out for seagulls! *Serves 4 to 6*

Accessories: 1 ramekin, 1 medium bowl

Board: 13-by-8-inch rectangle, wood

Caprese Salad

4 ounces mozzarella balls

½ cup cherry tomatoes, halved

3 fresh basil leaves, chopped

Balsamic glaze

For the Board

½ (5-ounce) package honeycomb

1 (6-ounce) wedge balsamic BellaVitano (cow's milk cheese)

2 handfuls rosemary, raisin, and pecan crisps or other sweet-and-savory crackers

1 cucumber, sliced

1 orange, sliced

2 bunches green grapes

1 handful blueberries

1 handful walnut pieces

2 fresh figs, halved

Edible flowers

1. **Make the Caprese Salad:** In a medium bowl, combine the mozzarella, tomatoes, and basil. Drizzle with balsamic glaze. Refrigerate until needed.

2. **Assemble the board:** Place a ramekin on the board and fill with honeycomb. Place the bowl of caprese salad on the board.

3. Place the BellaVitano on the board, opposite of the caprese bowl. Add the crisps, cucumber, orange, and grapes. Fill in the remaining space with blueberries, walnuts, and figs. Garnish with edible flowers.

My Perfect Bite: Rosemary, raisin, and pecan crisp, slice of cheese, spread of honeycomb, and half an orange slice.

Bottoms Up! When it comes to a hot summer day, I'm a spiked seltzer kind of girl. A citrus flavor would hit the spot with this board!

Honeycomb is nature's delicacy. It is not only beautiful but also edible! The creamy yet chewy consistency and delightfully sweet flavor is the perfect pairing for cheese. You can usually find honeycomb laying around the cheese selection at your local grocery store, but if you can't find it or aren't looking to splurge on it for this board, substitute it with a traditional wildflower honey and add a cute honey dipper for flare.

SUMMERTIME CITRUS, MOZZARELLA & PROSCIUTTO

Packed with the vibrant colors and tangy flavors of lemons, limes, grapefruits, and oranges, this board is the perfect treat poolside or after a long day on the lake! Don't skimp on the mint—it takes each bite to a whole new level. *Serves 4*

Board: 13-inch round, wood

2 lemons

2 limes

2 grapefruits

2 oranges

1 (8-ounce) ball fresh mozzarella, sliced

4 ounces prosciutto slices, folded

Extra-virgin olive oil

Freshly ground black pepper

Flaky sea salt

Mint leaves

1. Slice the citrus fruits into different shapes to add a variety of textures to the board. Make whole rounds, half-moons, and quarters to create a full, multidimensional look.

2. Arrange the slices of mozzarella on the board, placing one on top of the other, starting at the top of the board down to the bottom.

3. Layer the slices of citrus on the board. Use the whole rounds at the bottom and the smaller cuts toward the top.

4. Place the prosciutto on the board.

5. Drizzle everything with olive oil and sprinkle with pepper and salt. Garnish with mint leaves.

My Perfect Bite: A slice of fresh mozzarella paired with a sliver of prosciutto and a juicy piece of lemon. (Yes, lemon! I love the tangy, sour flavor paired with the creamy cheese.)

Bottoms Up! The orange and coriander aromas of a Belgian-style wheat ale pairs nicely with the citrus.

THE GRILL MASTER

●●○ $$$

This is the ultimate cookout board! Build your own burgers and hot dogs with the variety of toppings on this board. I've suggested my favorite condiments, but you can switch out or add yours. This board is perfect poolside or to remind Dad why he's the best on Father's Day.
Serves 4 to 6

Accessories: 5 ramekins, 1 medium bowl
Board: 20-by-13-inch rectangle, wood with rim

1 (16-ounce) package frozen fries
⅓ cup ketchup
⅓ cup mustard
⅓ cup mayonnaise
⅓ cup chili sauce
¼ cup pickle slices
2 cups prepared pasta salad
3 hamburger buns
3 hot dog buns
2 pretzel buns
3 cooked hamburgers or cheeseburgers
3 cooked hot dogs
3 pineapple rings
2 tomatoes, sliced
1 red onion, sliced
1 head butter lettuce, leaves separated

1. Cook the fries according to the package directions.

2. Place five ramekins and a medium bowl on the board. Fill the ramekins with the ketchup, mustard, mayonnaise, chili sauce, and pickles. Fill the bowl with pasta salad.

3. Place the hamburger buns, hot dog buns, and pretzel buns on the board. Add the cooked hamburgers directly to the center of the board. Place the hot dogs in the hot dog buns.

4. Fill in the remainder of the board with the pineapple, French fries, tomatoes, onion, and lettuce.

My Perfect Bite: A burger with everything, please! Load that baby up with all the fixings. Lettuce, tomato, onion, pickles, and all the condiments. Fries on the side!

Bottoms Up! Crack open an American craft classic, a Sierra Nevada Pale Ale.

If you want to take your pineapple rings up a notch, grill them over medium-high indirect heat for 5 to 7 minutes until they've caramelized.

ULTIMATE TACO TUESDAY

●●○ $$$

Whether it's Cinco de Mayo or Taco Tuesday, it's always the right time for tacos! Switch up my suggestions or add your favorite toppings and fillings to the board. You could even transform these ingredients into a loaded nachos board—the possibilities are endless!
Serves 4 to 6

Accessories: 2 ramekins, 5 small bowls, 1 medium bowl or mini cast-iron skillet

Board: 20-by-13-inch rectangle, wood with rim

4 to 6 flour or corn tortillas

1 cup fresh corn kernels or frozen roasted corn kernels, cooked and drained

1 (6-ounce) block Cotija

1 (6-ounce) block queso fresco

1 cup guacamole

2 Roma tomatoes, diced

⅓ cup sour cream

1 pound shredded chicken, cooked with taco seasoning

8 hard taco shells, warmed according to package directions

1 (8-ounce) package shredded lettuce

½ (10-ounce) package shredded red cabbage

1 small red onion, sliced

½ (8-ounce) package Mexican cheese blend

½ (16-ounce) bag tortilla chips

1 pound ground beef, cooked with taco seasoning

2 limes, sliced into wedges

1. Heat a large pan over medium-high heat and place the tortillas, one at a time or in batches, directly into the dry pan. Heat for about 45 seconds, until the bottoms are browned in spots. Keep warm in a basket or on a serving plate with a dish towel draped over them.

2. Place the medium bowl, the small bowls, and the ramekins across the board. Fill four of the bowls with the corn, Cotija, queso fresco, and guacamole. Fill the ramekins with the tomatoes and sour cream. Fill the fourth bowl with the chicken.

3. Fan the hard taco shells on either side of the board. Fill in the board with the lettuce, cabbage, onion, Mexican cheese blend, and tortilla chips.

4. Fill the medium bowl with the beef. Garnish with the lime wedges and serve the flour tortillas on the side.

My Perfect Bite: Hard taco shell, hefty scoop of sour cream (must be spread onto the bottom of the shell!), ground beef, shredded lettuce, diced tomatoes, sprinkle of Cotija, and a squeeze of lime juice.

Bottoms Up! A Spicy Cilantro Jalapeño Mezcal Margarita (page 173). Extra spicy for me, please!

Keep things easy and make your proteins according to the taco seasoning directions. Buy a rotisserie chicken or use the leftovers, which is a huge time-saver! If using fresh corn, try cooking it over medium heat in a nonstick skillet until browned and charred.

SUSHI BOARD

●○○ $$$

The at-home version of the sushi boat! If sushi wasn't already beautiful enough, this stylized display of your favorite rolls is an easy way make a five-star meal out of takeout.
Serves 2 to 4

Accessories: 1 ramekin, 2 medium bowls (plus more, if needed)
Board: 14-by-10-inch rectangle, wood

Your Takeout Order

Soy sauce

Edamame

Seaweed salad

Favorite dipping sauces, for serving (optional)

King crab rangoon

Pickled ginger

1 rainbow roll

1 tuna avocado roll

1 spicy crunchy crab roll

1 dreamy lobster roll

1 salmon roll

2 tuna sushi

2 salmon sushi

2 shrimp sushi

Wasabi

1. Place one ramekin on the board and pour in the soy sauce. Place the edamame and seaweed salad in the two medium bowls and set them on the side. Depending on the size of the board and the order, add additional ramekins and bowls for the other sauces or your sides.

2. Fan out the rangoon in the corner of the board. Add the pickled ginger to another corner of the board.

3. Begin arranging the sushi. I like to keep my sushi organized, but you can arrange your order however you'd like—in a fun shape, by color, in an alternating pattern—the possibilities are endless! Add the wasabi to the board where there is open space.

My Perfect Bite: I love the spicy crunchy crab roll, extra wasabi, dipped in soy sauce and finished off with a heaping bite of pickled ginger.

Bottoms Up! Try a sweeter white wine, like a Riesling. The semisweetness from the wine will offset the heat from the spicy sushi creating the perfect bite.

I use bakery boxes I found online, but you can also use disposable baking pans, food storage containers, or even a lunch box! Just make sure that your box has a raised edge to keep everything in place during travel.

WINERY TOUR TO-GO BOX

●●○ $$$

Headed to the winery? Surprise your friends with a snack board to go, filled with the perfect treats for your day between the vines. I recommend selecting mild, earthy cheeses like Brie, Camembert, and goat cheese, which pair well with ripe summer berries and most wines, ciders, and beers. (See page 188 for transportation tips.) *Serves 6 to 8*

Accessories: 1 honey dipper, wax paper

Board: 1 large and 1 small travel box

1 (2-ounce) jar honey

1 (1-ounce) jar wild blueberry or other fruit preserves

1 (1-ounce) jar stone-ground mustard

1 (6-ounce) wedge rosemary and olive oil Asiago or other herbed semisoft cheese

1 (8-ounce) round double crème Brie, cut into wedges

4 ounces prosciutto slices, folded

2 bunches green grapes

½ (16-ounce) package strawberries

1 (6-ounce) package blackberries

1 (6-ounce) package golden berries, golden raspberries, or dried apricots

½ kiwi

1 handful Marcona almonds

Rosemary sprigs

1 to 2 boxes crackers or crostini of choice

1. Place a sheet or two of wax paper on the bottom of a large box. This will ensure the food doesn't soak through the box. Place the honey, jam, and mustard jars in the box.

2. Place the Asiago in a corner of the box. Slice the bottom half of the cheese into ¼-inch pieces.

3. Starting at another corner, place the Brie wedges in a long connecting line. Place the folded prosciutto along the edge of the Brie.

4. Add the grapes, strawberries, blackberries, golden berries, kiwi, and almonds. Garnish with rosemary sprigs. Arrange the crackers in a smaller box.

My Perfect Bite: A wedge of creamy Brie on crostini, a light spread of wild blueberry preserves, and a few green grapes.

Bottoms Up! As many bottles of your favorite new wines as you can carry! A Riesling would pair beautifully, as would a hard cider or fruit beer.

SUMMER FLORAL

● ● ● $$$

Take your summer floral arrangement, but make it a snack board! This stunningly vivid and feminine board is perfect for summertime hosting. Take full advantage of the season's offerings by using fresh edible flowers to garnish your cheese (page 191) and selecting flavored preserves that mimic the flavors of the season. You can keep this board light and refreshing by using bright citrus and fresh cheeses. *Serves 6 to 8*

Accessories: 1 ramekin

Board: 13-inch round, wood

1 (5-ounce) round Boursin of choice

18 to 20 micro edible flowers

2 ounces tangerine preserves or orange marmalade

1 (7-ounce) round Comeback Cow or
  any soft cow's milk cheese

1 (6-ounce) wedge Manchego, sliced

1 to 2 handfuls water crackers

4 ounces prosciutto slices, folded

2 Genoa salami roses (page 194)

3 bunches green grapes

1 orange, sliced

1 to 2 handfuls raspberries

1 to 2 handfuls Marcona almonds

Thyme sprigs

1. Cover the Boursin in the edible flowers. For step-by-step directions, see page 191.

2. Place a ramekin on the board. Fill it with the tangerine preserves and garnish with an edible flower.

3. Place the Boursin and Comeback Cow cheeses on the board. Place one slice of Manchego on top of the other, alternating the direction of the slice to get a multidimensional look.

4. Add the crackers, placing them around the edges of the board and along one side of the Boursin.

5. Add the folded prosciutto and salami roses to the board. In the remaining space, place the grapes, orange slices, raspberries, and almonds. Garnish the board with thyme sprigs and edible flowers.

My Perfect Bite: Water cracker, slice of Manchego, spoonful of tangerine preserves, and a piece of prosciutto.

Bottoms Up! This board demands a colorful, fresh sangria.

If you can't find
Cabot clothbound
cheddar, slice up half
an 8-ounce block
of your favorite
cheddar variety.

RED, WHITE & BERRIES

Walk into your Independence Day party with this red, white, and blue board. Super simple ingredients, spectacular presentation! Choose a board with a rim and/or handles for easier transportation. (See page 188 for more travel tips.) *Serves 4 to 6*

Accessories: 1 ramekin, star-shaped cookie cutter (optional)

Board: 15-by-11-inch rectangle, wood with rim

1 (4-ounce) wedge Cabot clothbound cheddar, cut into ¼-inch-thick slices

1 pound cherries

½ (8-ounce) wedge blueberry Wensleydale (fresh sheep's or cow's milk cheese) or any fruity cheese, cut into ¼-inch-thick slices

1 (12-ounce) package blackberries

6 ounces bresaola slices, folded

2 to 3 handfuls sesame crackers

1 (12-ounce) package blueberries

⅓ cup plum jam

1. If desired, cut the cheddar slices into star shapes using a star-shaped cookie cutter. If you don't have a star-shaped cookie cutter, you can halve the slices diagonally for visual interest.

2. In a straight row, add the cherries to the bottom of the board. Above the cherries, add a row of the sliced Wensleydale and the cheddar. For the third row, add the blackberries. For the fourth row, add the folded bresaola. For the fifth row, add the crackers. For the sixth and last row, add the blueberries.

3. Serve plum jam on the side in a ramekin.

My Perfect Bite: Sesame cracker, piece of cheddar, plum jam, and a blackberry.

Bottoms Up! Pair with a July Fourth classic: fresh-squeezed lemonade. Add a few fresh blueberries for some festive fun!

S'MORE, PLEASE!

The combinations are endless with this board. Try the warm s'mores dip on top of a peanut butter cup, or make a chocolate pretzel s'mores sandwich—you can't go wrong whichever way you choose. And the best part is, there's no fire needed! *Serves 4 to 6*

Accessories: 1 small ovenproof dish or mini cast-iron skillet

Board: 12-by-11-inch rectangle, wood

S'mores Dip

3 full-size milk chocolate bars, broken into pieces

1½ cups mini marshmallows

For the Board

8 to 12 graham crackers

2 to 4 chocolate chip cookies

2 handfuls chocolate-covered pretzels

2 full-size milk chocolate bars, broken into squares

2 full-size cookies 'n' cream chocolate bars, broken into squares

5 to 6 peanut butter cups

6 to 8 strawberries, halved

1. Preheat the oven to 350°F. Set a placeholder on the board for the dip dish.

2. **Make the S'mores Dip:** Place the chocolate pieces into the dish and top with the marshmallows. Bake for 5 to 6 minutes, or until the marshmallows are browned. While it's baking, assemble the board.

3. **Assemble the board:** Place the graham crackers, chocolate chip cookies, and pretzels on the board. Add the milk chocolate squares, cookies n' cream squares, peanut butter cups, and strawberries.

4. Remove the placeholder and replace it with a trivet or folded paper towel to protect your board from the heat. Carefully add the dip to the board.

My Perfect Bite: A big scoop of s'mores dip on a graham cracker topped with a fresh strawberry.

Bottoms Up! I'd pair this sweet, rich board with a spicy bourbon cocktail, like a Vanilla Old-Fashioned (page 172). The perfect cocktail for a faux-fireside evening!

Mini marshmallows get gooey and brown quicker than larger ones, so the chocolate is less likely to burn.

DIY ICE CREAM SUNDAES

You scream, I scream, they'll all scream for this board! Keep the kids busy with this perfect DIY dessert or make any summer day a Sundae Funday because this board is fun for the whole family. Grab your favorite ice cream toppings, and make this board your own! *Serves 6*

Accessories: 1 ramekin, 4 small bowls
Board: 20-by-13-inch rectangle, wood with rim

1 (10-ounce) jar maraschino cherries

⅓ cup rainbow sprinkles

1 (11.5-ounce) jar caramel sauce

1 (11.5-ounce) jar chocolate fudge

3 to 6 sugar cones

3 to 6 waffle bowls

3 to 4 handfuls chocolate-covered pretzels

3 to 4 handfuls mini chocolate cookies

1 (10-ounce) package M&M's

1 (10-ounce) package mini peanut butter cups

1 (8-ounce) package gummy bears

2 (4-ounce) cans roasted peanuts

1 pint chocolate ice cream

1 pint strawberry ice cream

1 pint vanilla ice cream

1. Save space for the ice cream pints using three small bowls or cans. Keep the ice cream in the freezer until you're ready to serve.

2. Add a fourth small bowl and a ramekin to the board. Fill the bowl with the cherries and the ramekin with the sprinkles. Add the jars of caramel sauce and chocolate fudge. Place the sugar cones and waffles bowls on either side of the board.

3. Arrange the pretzels and chocolate cookies around the ramekins. Fill the remainder of the board with the M&M's, peanut butter cups, gummy bears, and roasted peanuts.

4. Swap in the ice cream right before serving. Give it about 5 minutes to come to temperature so that it's easier to scoop.

My Perfect Bite: A bowl of maraschino cherries with some ice cream on top, please! I'm kidding . . . but not really.

Bottoms Up! You can easily transform this board into the perfect a root beer float! Grab a can of your favorite root beer and top 'er off!

Want to make it boozy? Make a frozen mudslide with one part coffee liqueur, one part vodka, one part Irish cream liqueur, all on top of vanilla ice cream and chocolate fudge!

4
FALL

AFTERNOON PICK-ME-UP

●○○ $$$

Put a little pep in your step with this coffee-inspired board. Filled with some of my favorite sweet and savory snacks, it's sure to help you make it through the afternoon slump.
Serves 4 to 6

Accessories: 2 ramekins

Board: 13-by-8-inch rectangle, wood

¼ cup raw sugar

⅓ cup black cherry jam or jam of choice

1 (6-ounce) wedge espresso BellaVitano (cow's milk cheese)

1 (6-ounce) wedge aged Gouda, sliced

3 pistachio biscotti or biscotti of choice

5 butter shortbread cookies

6 dark chocolate–covered cookie sticks

6 chocolate and hazelnut créme wafers

1 (6-ounce) package blueberries

1 to 2 handfuls kiwi berries or other small fruit, halved

2 handfuls pumpkin-spice or chocolate-covered espresso beans

1 to 2 cups walnut pieces

1 to 2 handfuls pomegranate seeds

Rosemary sprigs

1. Place two ramekins on either side of the board. Fill one with the sugar and the other with the jam. Place the BellaVitano and Gouda on opposites sides of the board, fanning out the Gouda slices through the center.

2. Around the edges of the board, layer the biscotti, shortbread cookies, cookie sticks, and wafers on the board. Add the blueberries, kiwi berries, and espresso beans. Fill any remaining space with walnuts and pomegranate seeds. Garnish with rosemary sprigs.

My Perfect Bite: Slice of espresso BellaVitano over pistachio biscotti with a schmear of black cherry jam and a few pomegranate seeds.

Bottoms Up! A classic cappuccino with a sprinkle of cinnamon!

The BellaVitano is hand-rubbed with freshly roasted espresso! It's the perfect pairing with the sweet aged cheese, which offers flavors of butterscotch, cream, and toasted nuts. It's great any time of the day, but I love this cheese in the morning. If you aren't able to find it, no worries! You can substitute with any aged, crumbly cheese.

FALL HARVEST

●●● $$$

Designed to highlight the flavors of the season and colors of the falling leaves, this board will surely impress. The extra special Brie Brûlée adds a rich, caramelized flavor to the cheese that is truly unforgettable! *Serves 8 to 10*

Accessories: 1 ramekin, 1 mini pumpkin or gourd, 1 mini kitchen torch (optional)

Board: 16-inch round, wood with handles

Brie Brûlée

1 round double crème Brie

1 tablespoon superfine sugar, plus 1 teaspoon

For the Board

3 tablespoons cherry-cabernet jam or cherry jam

1 (8-ounce) wedge creamy cinnamon Toscano or cinnamon-dusted cheddar Parmesan, sliced

1 (6-ounce) log cranberry-cinnamon goat cheese, such as Celebrity brand, sliced

3 small bunches red grapes

5 candied orange slices

½ pomegranate

1 Bosc pear, sliced

3 to 4 handfuls beet crackers

4 ounces Chianti salami slices

6 ounces prosciutto slices, folded

2 fresh figs, halved

½ (6-ounce) package golden berries or dried apricots

1 cup Candied Nuts (page 145), or store-bought

Oregano sprigs

Edible flowers

1. **Make the Brie Brûlée:** Slice off the top layer of the Brie's rind. Top the Brie with 1 tablespoon of sugar until completed covered. Use a miniature kitchen torch to slowly melt the sugar by evenly moving the torch back and forth until the sugar begins to bubble and crust. Add the remaining 1 teaspoon of sugar and repeat the process to form a thick crust.

2. **Assemble the board:** Place the mini pumpkin, pomegranate half, and a ramekin on the board. Fill the ramekin with jam. Add the Brie, Toscano, and goat cheeses. Arrange the grapes, orange slices, and pear on the board.

3. Add the crackers, salami, and proscuitto slices. Fill in the board with the figs, golden berries, and pecans. Garnish the board with oregano sprigs and edible flowers.

My Perfect Bite: A wedge of Brie Brûlée spread on a cracker with a dollop of jam.

Bottoms Up! Enjoy with a glass or two of Autumn Harvest Punch (page 174)—the perfect party punch for your seasonal gatherings!

Don't have a mini torch? I implore you to buy one. They're so much fun and aren't **that** dangerous— I kid. But really, they aren't too expensive on Amazon and come in handy more than you might think. If you aren't up for it this time, pop the Brie under the broiler for 5 to 6 minutes, or until the top is caramelized and crispy. This might make the cheese a bit melty, so I recommend serving it in an ovenproof dish, not directly on the board.

OOEY-GOOEY FONDUE-Y

●●● $$$

Who needs the Melting Pot? You can warm up with this epic fondue board in the comfort of your own home when the weather starts to get chilly. Experiment with your dippers—pretty much anything tastes delicious covered in cheese, right? *Serves 8*

Accessories: 1 fondue pot and 8 fondue forks, or a medium heat-safe dish and 8 wooden skewers

Board: 16-by-14-inch rectangle, wood

Rosemary Roasted Potatoes

10 to 12 small potatoes, halved

3 tablespoons olive oil

3 garlic cloves, minced

2 tablespoons fresh rosemary leaves

Flaky sea salt

Freshly ground black pepper

Classic Swiss Fondue

1 garlic clove, halved

1 (6-ounce) block Gruyère, grated

1 (6-ounces) block Emmentaler, grated

1 (4-ounce) wedge Appenzeller, grated

2 tablespoons cornstarch

1 cup dry white wine

1 tablespoon Dijon mustard

1 teaspoon lemon juice

Freshly ground black pepper

Pinch ground nutmeg

For the Board

1 loaf ciabatta bread

2 cups broccoli florets, steamed

6 to 7 rainbow carrots

1 cucumber

2 Granny Smith apples

4 ounces chorizo slices

4 to 5 fresh figs

1 to 2 handfuls cherry tomatoes

Rosemary sprigs

To steam the broccoli, fill a saucepan with one inch of water. Place a steamer basket on top. Put the broccoli in the steamer, then bring the water to a boil and steam for 5 to 6 minutes, or until the broccoli is fork-tender. You can also opt to serve the broccoli raw if you prefer!

continued »

1. Preheat the oven to 400°F.

2. **Make the Rosemary Roasted Potatoes:** In a large bowl, combine the potatoes, olive oil, garlic, and rosemary. Season to taste with salt and pepper. Toss until the potatoes are well coated. Spread the potatoes evenly on a rimmed baking sheet and roast for at least 40 minutes, stirring once, or until browned and crisp.

3. While the potatoes are cooking, prepare the other ingredients. Cube the bread, halve the carrots, slice the cucumber, dice the apples, slice the chorizo, and halve the figs. Set aside while you make the fondue.

4. **Make the Classic Swiss Fondue:** Rub the inside of a fondue pot or a saucepan with the halved garlic clove, then discard. In a medium bowl, toss the Gruyère, Emmentaler, and Appenzeller with the cornstarch and coat completely. Transfer the cheese mixture to the fondue pot. Add the wine, mustard, and lemon juice and cook over medium heat until the cheeses begin to melt. Add a generous pinch each of pepper and nutmeg and cook, stirring gently, until creamy and smooth.

5. **Assemble the board:** Place the fondue pot in the center of the board. (If you're not using a fondue pot, transfer the fondue into a cocotte or any heat-safe serving bowl.) Place the ciabatta around the pot so that they absorb the heat. Next, add the broccoli, potatoes, carrots, cucumbers, apples, chorizo, figs, and tomatoes. Garnish with rosemary sprigs.

My Perfect Bite: I'd eat a piece of tree bark if it was dipped in this fondue. Everything and anything can be a perfect bite!

Bottoms Up! Enjoy with a kirsch (morello cherry brandy) cocktail as an after-dinner digestif.

GOURMET GRILLED CHEESE & TOMATO SOUP

●●● $$$

Although a traditional grilled cheese will hold a special place in any child's heart, it is never too late to spice up an old classic. This board offers three different gourmet grilled cheeses that will have you fighting over the last crumb! These are a few of my personal favorite combos, but feel free to make any sandwiches that fit your family's preferences. I use one loaf of ciabatta and one loaf pumpernickel for this board, which is enough for the sandwiches and to have extra pieces left over for dipping.
Serves 6 to 8

Accessories: 1 medium or large bowl, 1 small bowl
Board: 20-by-12-inch rectangle, slate

Spicy Garlic & Four Cheese Grilled Cheese

- 4 ciabatta bread slices
- 3 tablespoons melted butter
- 1 tablespoon finely chopped fresh parsley
- 1 tablespoon garlic powder
- Pinch freshly ground black pepper
- ½ cup grated habanero cheddar or other spicy melting cheese
- ¼ cup shredded Parmesan
- ¼ cup shredded Gruyère
- ½ cup shredded mozzarella

Apple Butter & Brie Grilled Cheese

- 4 sourdough bread slices
- 4 tablespoons apple butter
- 1 (8-ounce) round triple crème Brie, thinly sliced
- 1 apple, thinly sliced

Pear & Fontina Grilled Cheese

- 2 tablespoons butter
- 4 pumpernickel bread slices
- 2 tablespoons Dijon mustard
- 1 cup shredded fontina
- 1 Bartlett pear, thinly sliced
- 4 crispy prosciutto slices

For the Board

- 3 cups tomato soup
- Fine sea salt
- Freshly ground black pepper
- 2 tablespoons heavy cream (optional)
- 1 cup croutons (optional)
- 1 (8-ounce) wedge Manchego, sliced
- 1 blood orange or regular orange, sliced
- 2 pears, sliced
- 2 apples, sliced
- 1 handful walnuts
- 1 handful hazlenuts
- Basil leaves

continued »

1. Preheat the oven to 375°F. Line a large baking sheet with parchment paper.

2. **Make the Spicy Garlic & Four Cheese Grilled Cheese:** Place the ciabatta slices on the prepared baking sheet. In a small bowl, thoroughly mix together the butter, parsley, garlic powder, and pepper. In a medium bowl, mix together the cheddar, Parmesan, Gruyère, and mozzarella. Spread the butter mixture evenly on one side of each slice of ciabatta. Place a handful of the cheese mixture on each slice of bread. Set face up on the baking sheet.

3. **Make the Apple Butter & Brie Grilled Cheese:** Place the ciabatta slices on the prepared baking sheet. Spread one side of each slice with apple butter. Layer the slices of Brie on each piece of bread and top one slice with apple slices. Set face up on the baking sheet.

4. **Make the Pear & Fontina Grilled Cheese:** Butter one side of each pumpernickel slice. Place each slice, buttered-side down, on a plate. Spread each slice with the mustard. Place a small handful of fontina on each of the four slices. Top two of the slices with the pear and prosciutto. Top each with one of the other slices to create the sandwiches. Set aside.

5. Place the baking sheet of sandwich halves in oven and cook for 6 to 8 minutes, or until the cheese has fully melted.

6. Meanwhile, in a medium saucepan, warm the tomato soup over medium-low heat. Season to taste with salt and pepper. If using, add the cream to the soup. Set aside.

7. Heat a medium skillet over medium heat. Pan-fry the fontina grilled cheese on each side until lightly browned and the cheese is melty.

8. **Assemble the board:** Place a medium to large bowl and a small bowl on the board. Fill the larger bowl with hot soup and the smaller one with croutons, if using. Fan the Manchego slices around the soup bowl.

9. Cut the sandwiches in half and layer them across the center of the board, placing one on top of the other.

10. Place the orange, pear, and apple slices around the edges of the board. Fill in any open spaces with the walnuts and hazlenuts. Garnish with basil leaves.

My Perfect Bite: I'm grabbing a Spicy Garlic & Four Cheese sandwich and taking it for a swim in the tomato soup.

Bottoms Up! Try a medium-bodied red wine like Chianti. The red fruity notes and bright acidity in this wine make it a great pairing for the creamy tomato soup and toasty sandwiches.

You can crisp up your prosciutto by baking it at 375°F for 8 to 10 minutes. If you're feeling extra fancy, use your leftover bread to make homemade croutons. Cube the remaining bread and combine in a bowl with olive oil, sea salt and freshly cracked black pepper. Bake in the oven at 375°F for about 5 to 6 minutes, or until crispy and golden.

SPICE, SPICE, BABY

●●● $$$

Put your heat tolerance to the test with this board. Fair warning: It's not for the faint of heart! The hot honey on this board takes everything up a notch. *Serves 6 to 8*

Accessories: 1 ramekin, 1 small ovenproof dish or mini cast-iron skillet

Board: 11-inch square, wood

Bacon & Cayenne Baked Brie

4 bacon slices, diced

1 cup packed light brown sugar

2 tablespoons honey

1 teaspoon ground cayenne pepper

1 teaspoon red pepper flakes

⅛ teaspoon ground nutmeg

1 (8-ounce) round Brie

For the Board

¼ cup hot honey

1 (7-ounce) block habanero ghost pepper Monterey Jack, or any spicy cheese, sliced

½ French baguette, sliced

2 ounces soppressata slices

2 ounces calabrese salami slices, folded

2 to 3 handfuls pretzel crisps

1 (6-ounce) jar Manzanilla olives

2 to 3 handfuls sriracha almonds or other spicy nuts

1 red pepper, halved

1 red apple, sliced

It's super easy to make your hot honey! Combine 2 tablespoons of red pepper flakes with 1 cup of honey in a small pot over medium-high heat. Bring the mixture to a gentle simmer. Then remove from the heat.

Allow the red pepper flakes to infuse the honey for 5 to 10 minutes. Then remove them with a fine-mesh sieve, if desired, or leave the red pepper flakes in the honey for an increased kick over time. Transfer the honey to an airtight, heat-safe container. Store in a cool, dry place at room temperature for up to 6 months—and make sure to use it in the Spicy Fried Goat Cheese Balls on page 151.

continued »

1. **Make the Bacon & Cayenne Baked Brie:**
   Preheat the oven to 350°F. In a medium skillet, cook the bacon over medium heat until crispy. Pour off the excess bacon fat. Add the brown sugar, honey, cayenne, red pepper flakes, and nutmeg to the pan. Mix to combine. Place the Brie in a small ovenproof dish and use a sharp knife to score the top of the Brie in a checkered pattern. Pour the bacon topping over the Brie and bake for 15 minutes, or until the Brie is gooey. When ready to plate, carefully dish and enjoy immediately.

2. **Assemble the board:** While the Brie is baking, place a ramekin and a placeholder for the Brie on the board. Fill the ramekin with hot honey.

3. Add the Monterey Jack to the board by fanning out the slices around the hot honey.

4. Place the baguette slices around where the Brie will set. This will allow them to absorb the heat from the pan and protect the rest of the ingredients. Add the soppressata and salami to the board. Fill in the board with the pretzel crisps, olives, almonds, and pepper.

5. Once the Brie is finished, place a trivet or folded paper towel on the board to protect it from the heat. Transfer the baked Brie to the board. Drizzle hot honey over the top before serving. Serve the apple on the side.

My Perfect Bite: A healthy scoop of baked Brie on baguette, followed up with a bite of crisp apple.

Bottoms Up! Cool down with a chilled glass of a fuller-bodied rosé.

TOIL & TREATS

●●● $$$

This board proves that Halloween isn't all about the candy! I carved a skull from the Brie by hand, but you can use a cookie cutter to make your own spooky designs—you could even leave it whole and add googly eyes. I chose cheeses with dark, spooky coloring, but feel free to make this your interpretation of Halloween. *Serves 8 to 10*

Accessories: 1 ramekin, 1 small bowl or mini witch's cauldron, wax paper

Board: 15-inch round, wood with rim

Witch's Cauldron Blueberry Bubbles

1 (6-ounce) package blueberries

1 cup green candy melts

2 tablespoons coarse sugar

Spooky Olive Eyeballs

Edible googly eyes

5 ounces pitted Castelvetrano olives

For the Board

1 (8-ounce) round double crème Brie

1 (6- ounce) wedge merlot BellaVitano (cow's milk cheese), sliced

2 (4-ounce) logs blueberry-vanilla goat cheese, sliced

3 bunches purple grapes

2 to 3 handfuls fig-and-olive crackers

10 ounces calabrese salami slices, folded

1 (6-ounce) package blackberries

1 to 2 handfuls butter toffee almonds or other nuts

3 to 4 candied orange slices, halved

2 tablespoons plum spread (optional)

2 fresh figs, halved

4 rosemary sprigs

Ghost-shaped potato chips, such as from Trader Joe's (optional)

How stinkin' cute are those edible googly eyes on the next page? I found them on Amazon, and one small container comes with more than enough for this board. Better yet, they come in two different sizes, which is perfect for creating a variety of tiny monsters!

continued »

1. **Make the Witch's Cauldron Blueberry Bubbles:** Wash and dry blueberries and lay them out in a single layer on wax paper. Microwave the green candy melts until silky and smooth. Transfer to a resealable bag. Cut a small hole into the corner of the bag with a pair of sharp scissors. Drizzle the melted candy over the blueberries, then sprinkle with the sugar. Allow to cool for at least 1 hour or refrigerate for 20 minutes, until the candy has hardened. Set aside.

2. **Make the Spooky Olive Eyeballs:** Add the googly eyes to the olives by lightly pressing the eye into the opening on the olive. If your olives aren't pitted, apply a bit more pressure so that the eye is suctioned onto the olive. Set aside.

3. **Assemble the board:** Place a ramekin and the small bowl on the board. On opposite sides of the board, place the Brie, BellaVitano, and goat cheese.

4. Add the grapes, crackers, and calabrese slices around the ramekin and cauldron. Fill the remaining space on the board with the blackberries, almonds, and orange slices. If you've carved the Brie into a skull, fill the eye sockets with the plum spread. Add the blueberry bubbles to the cauldron and the olive eyeballs to the ramekin.

5. Garnish with the figs, rosemary sprigs, and ghost-shaped potato chips, if using. For a little extra spookiness, add a few googly eyes to your figs, too!

My Perfect Bite: A fig-and-olive cracker with a wedge of skull Brie with plum spread, slice of calabrese salmi, and a candied orange half.

Bottoms Up! Snack on this board while you sip a Witch's Brew (page 178).

GAME DAY BOARD

●●○ $$$

A quick and easy board for a day full of yelling at a TV screen! You might get angry, but at least you won't be hungry. This is my go-to board for snacking by the big screen and is filled with everything you need—crunchy chips, spicy boneless wings, and ooey-gooey cheese! Need I say more? *Serves 6 to 8*

Accessories: 2 small bowls

Board: 15-inch round, wood with rim

18 to 20 frozen boneless buffalo-style chicken bites

10 frozen breaded mozzarella sticks

⅓ cup ranch dressing

⅓ cup marinara sauce

½ (8-ounce) block Vermont sharp cheddar, sliced

1 recipe Spicy Fried Goat Cheese Balls (page 151) or ½ (12-ounce) package marinated mozzarella balls

3 ounces Italian dry salami slices

3 to 4 carrots, cut into sticks, or 10 to 15 baby carrots

3 to 4 celery stalks, cut into sticks

6 to 8 pepperoncini

2 handfuls potato chips

1 (6-ounce) can sriracha almonds (optional)

1. Cook the chicken bites and mozzarella sticks according to package directions.

2. Place two small bowls on the board. Fill one with the ranch dressing and the other with the marinara sauce. Fan the cheddar slices, placing one on top of the other, around one of the bowls.

3. Add the chicken bites, goat cheese balls, and mozzarella sticks to the board.

4. Fill the remaining space on the board with the salami, carrots, celery, pepperoncini, and potato chips. Serve the sriracha almonds on the side, if using.

My Perfect Bite: I will guard these fried cheese balls with my life. I'm telling you: don't sleep on them! They're a must-have on game day.

Bottoms Up! A slightly sweet, slightly spiced Belgian-style blonde ale is the perfect pairing for this board.

THAI TAKEOUT IT UP A NOTCH

●○○ $$$

Whether you're having company over and aren't up for cooking or you're planning on a Saturday night in, this is the perfect guide to creating a impressive spread in minutes. Call in an order at your favorite restaurant and take your takeout up a notch with this beautiful presentation of fuss-free food. *Serves 4*

Accessories: 2 ramekins, 2 small
  bowls, chopsticks (optional)
Board: 14-by-10-inch rectangle, wood,
  and 11-by-7-inch rectangle, wood

Your Takeout Order

1 papaya salad with
  dressing

2 vegetable spring rolls

2 curry puffs

2 pieces beef satay

1 order mango and sticky
  rice

1 order red curry chicken

1 order shrimp pad Thai

1 order jasmine rice

8 pieces fried tofu

4 chicken wings

2 steamed dumplings

2 pieces chicken satay

Garnishes

Cilantro sprigs (optional)

Peanuts (optional)

Save the takeout container and serve the rice right from the box. It will keep your rice warm and add a super cute takeout touch. Check out the Sushi Board (page 68) for another way to fancify your takeout!

1. Grab two boards or serving platters: a smaller one for appetizers and a larger one for entrées.

2. On the appetizer board, place a ramekin. Fill it with the dressing from the papaya salad and surround the bowl with the salad. Add a few other appetizer items to the board, like the spring rolls, curry puffs, and beef satay.

3. On the entrée board, in each corner, place a ramekin. Fill one with the sauce for the sticky rice and the other with the sauce for the tofu, dumplings, and spring rolls. Leave the corners surrounding them free for now.

4. Add a small bowl and fill it with the chicken curry. Spread the pad Thai evenly across the middle of the board. (Make sure that shrimp is front and center!) Begin to build around the pad Thai with the jasmine rice (leave it in the box for extra flair!), fried tofu, chicken wings, dumplings, and chicken satay.

5. Add the mango slices and sticky rice to the remaining corner of the board. Garnish with cilantro sprigs and peanuts, if using.

My Perfect Bite: A scoop of red chicken curry and vegetables over warm jasmine rice.

Bottoms Up! A traditional Thai iced tea! This sweet and creamy-yet-refreshing tea has flavors of star anise, crushed tamarind, and cardamom that pair perfectly with your meal.

OKTOBERFEST

●●○ $$$

This spectacular German festival, and world's largest folk fest, has inspired a worldwide phenomenon celebrating Bavarian culture. Filled with good food, great beer, and lots of dancing on tables, who wouldn't want to recreate this in their own home? This board is a homage to the Munich festival and full of delicious food to celebrate the occasion, even if you are thousands of miles away! *Serves 8 to 10*

Accessories: 2 ramekins, 2 medium bowls
Board: 20-by-15-inch rectangle, wood

6 to 8 frozen salted soft pretzels

2 cups prepared German potato salad

1 (8-ounce) container beer cheese spread

⅓ cup sauerkraut

¼ cup Dijon mustard

3 to 4 cooked smoked sausage links

3 brioche bratwurst buns

3 to 4 cooked bratwursts

1 (10-ounce) wedge aged Gouda, sliced

1 (8-ounce) block Muenster, cubed

3 bunches champagne grapes or other grapes

3 to 4 handfuls hard pretzels

Parsley sprigs

1. Prepare the pretzels according to the package instructions. While the pretzels are baking, assemble the board.

2. Place two medium bowls and two ramekins on the board. Fill the bowls with the potato salad and beer cheese. Fill the ramekins with the sauerkraut and mustard.

3. Starting at one corner, place the soft pretzels, slightly layering them, down the board. Layer the smoked sausage in another corner, giving them some height. Put the buns in another corner and place the bratwurst inside.

4. Place the Gouda and Muenster on opposite sides of the board. Fill in the remaining space with the grapes and pretzels. Garnish with parsley sprigs.

My Perfect Bite: A warm, salted piece of soft pretzel smothered in Bavarian beer cheese spread.

Bottoms Up! Enjoy this board with a refreshing German wheat beer, like the iconic Paulaner hefeweizen, bottled in Munich itself!

THANKSGIVING LEFTOVERS

●○○ $$$

Whether as a late-night snack or Friday's lunch, this board is a fun way to dress up what's left of everyone's favorite feast! Your needs will depend on your leftovers, but this should give you a good starting point. This is my family's favorite part of the holiday . . . second dinner! *Serves 6 to 8*

Accessories: 2 ramekins, 2 small bowls, 1 medium bowl or mini cast-iron skillet

Board: 20-by-15-inch rectangle, wood

2 to 3 cups stuffing

1 to 2 cups mashed sweet potatoes

1 cup cranberry sauce

¼ cup Dijon mustard

¼ cup mayonnaise

8 slices leftover turkey breast

6 to 7 Hawaiian sweet rolls or other sandwich rolls

1 (8-ounce) wedge Emmi Swiss Raclette

2 handfuls cranberry-and-hazelnut crisps

2 bunches red grapes

½ pomegranate

1 head green leaf lettuce, leaves separated

1 (6-ounce) package blackberries

1½ cups walnut pieces

3 fresh figs, halved

3 rosemary sprigs

Gravy, for serving

1. Warm up all your leftovers.

2. Place the medium bowl, two smaller bowls, and two ramekins on the board. Fill the medium bowl with the stuffing. Fill the two smaller bowls with the sweet potatoes and cranberry sauce, then fill the two ramekins with the mustard and mayonnaise.

3. Fan out the sliced turkey around the stuffing. Create two little piles of rolls, placing the rolls on top of each other.

4. Place the Raclette in the bottom corner and fan out the crisps on either side of the board. Add the grapes and pomegranate.

5. Fill in the remaining space with the lettuce, blackberries, walnuts, and figs. Garnish with rosemary sprigs. Serve the gravy on the side.

My Perfect Bite: Turkey, a spoonful of stuffing, lettuce, mayo, and mustard on a roll.

Bottoms Up! A full-bodied brown ale adds the complexity of dry, nuttiness to your sandwich. Try a Dogfish Head Indian Brown Ale!

THANKFUL FOR DESSERTS

●●○ $$$

Pumpkin spice and everything nice! It's fall, and that means it's officially pie season. This board is the perfect way wrap up a cozy fall meal or, better yet, send off a Thanksgiving feast! The best part is, all of these delicious desserts are store-bought! Shh . . . no one needs to know. *Serves 8 to 10*

Accessories: 1 small bowl
Board: 17-inch round, wood

Pumpkin Spice Whipped Cream

1 cup heavy cream

¼ cup powdered sugar

1 teaspoon pumpkin pie spice

1 teaspoon pure vanilla extract

For the Board

1 large pecan pie

2 mini pumpkin pies

4 glazed pumpkin donuts

1 to 2 handfuls maple leaf cookies

1 to 2 handfuls gingersnap cookies

4 to 6 dried orange slices (page 166) or store-bought

10 ounces dark chocolate almond bark, broken into pieces

2 to 3 handfuls cinnamon–brown sugar pretzel pieces or Candied Nuts (page 145)

1 to 2 handfuls chewy caramels

1 to 2 handfuls pomegranate clusters or pomegranate seeds

1 to 2 handfuls seasonal chocolates

Thyme sprigs

1. **Make the Pumpkin Spice Whipped Cream:** In a large bowl, combine the heavy cream, sugar, pumpkin pie spice, and vanilla extract. With an electric mixer on medium-high speed, mix until stiff peaks form, about 4 to 5 minutes. Store in the fridge until you're ready to serve.

2. **Assemble the board:** Place the pecan pie, pumpkin pies, donuts, and a small bowl on the board. Cut one or two slices out of the pecan pie.

3. Layer in the maple leaf cookies, placing one on top of the other, around the pecan pie. Add the gingersnaps and orange slices. Fill in the remaining space with almond bark, pretzel pieces, and caramels.

4. Place the whipped cream in the bowl. Place a dollop of whipped cream on the mini pumpkin pies and garnish with the pomegranate clusters, chocolates, and thyme sprigs.

My Perfect Bite: A bite of pumpkin pie, a heaping spoonful whipped cream, and a pomegranate cluster.

Bottoms Up! Grab an autumn ale. This full-bodied old ale offers a delicate blend of Bavarian hops with a nutty-sweet middle that works well with sweet fall flavors.

To make pomegranate clusters, score around the pomegranate fruit and peel back the skin, revealing the individual fruit sections. Gently break apart the individual fruit sections, trying to keep the clusters of seeds intact. Pick out large clusters of seeds and peel off any excess pith.

4
WINTER

BUILD-A-BAGEL BOARD

● ○ ○ $$$

Did you know that February 9 is National Bagel Day? Another winter holiday worth celebrating! Everyone has their own idea of the perfect bagel toppings, and this is an easy way make sure everyone can build their perfect breakfast. This board is super easy to customize for different dietary concerns: include gluten-free bagels, tofu cream cheese—the sky's the limit. *Serves 6*

Accessories: 2 small bowls, 1 ramekin

Board: 16-by-14-inch rectangle, wood

1 (7.5-ounce) package chive and onion cream cheese

1 (7.5-ounce) package garden vegetable cream cheese

¼ cup capers

6 assorted fresh bagels, halved

2 tomatoes, sliced

1 cucumber, sliced

2 to 3 handfuls arugula

2 bunches grapes

1 red onion, sliced

8 crispy bacon slices

2 (4-ounce) packages smoked salmon

1 lemon, sliced

1 (6-ounce) package blueberries

3 to 4 strawberries, halved

Lemon rind flower (optional)

1. Place two small bowls and a ramekin on the board. Fill one bowl with the chive and onion cream cheese and the other with the garden vegetable cream cheese. Fill the ramekin with the capers.

2. Layer the bagels on top of one another in the center of the board, alternating flavors.

3. Surround the bagels with toppings, starting with the tomato slices, then the cucumber slices, arugula, grapes, and onion. Add the bacon, smoked salmon, lemon slices, blueberries, and strawberries. Garnish with a lemon rind flower, if using.

My Perfect Bite: Everything bagel, chive and onion cream cheese, arugula, bacon, tomato, red onion, with freshly ground black pepper and sea salt.

Bottoms Up! Nothing is better than bagels and coffee. Pair this board with a tall cup o' joe.

To make a lemon rind flower, use a sharp knife or vegetable peeler and peel the yellow rind (do not include any white part) in a continuous strip from the lemon. Curl the strip in a circle, yellow-side out, as tightly as possible without breaking it. Hold it together with a toothpick, if needed.

GINGERBREAD
COCOA MIX
NET WT 1 OZ (28g)

THE MODERN GOURMET
TOASTED
MARSHMALLOW
COCOA MIX
NATURALLY & ARTIFICIALLY FLAVORED
NET WT 1 OZ (28g)

PEPPER
COCO

D CARAMEL
COA MIX

You can buy bags of already
crushed candy canes or do it
yourself. I crushed about six
candy canes for this amount.

COZY HOT COCOA BOARD

●○○ $$$

Now this is my kind of snow day! Throw on your favorite holiday movie and leave the shoveling for tomorrow. I added different hot cocoa mixes to my board so people could choose their favorites, but you can also make a big batch of cocoa on the stovetop and save the board for all the toppings. *Serves 5*

Accessories: 2 medium bowls, 4 ramekins, 2 hot cocoa mugs (optional)

Board: 17-inch round, wood

1 (8-ounce) package mini marshmallows

8 holiday marshmallow cocoa toppers or large marshmallows

2 to 3 handfuls white chocolate–covered pretzels

2 to 3 handfuls peppermint candies

1 to 2 handfuls peppermint white chocolate truffles, such as Lindt brand

1 (3.5-ounce) bar dark chocolate peppermint bark

8 candy canes

½ cup white chocolate chips

½ cup milk chocolate chips

1 oz red, white, and green nonpareils

1 (3-ounce) package Sno-Caps

⅓ cup crushed candy canes

1 cup shredded coconut

Whipped cream, for serving

1. Place two medium bowls and four ramekins on the board. Add two hot cocoa mugs, if using.

2. Pile the marshmallows high on about a quarter of the board. Place the marshmallow cocoa toppers, pretzels, peppermint candies, truffles, peppermint bark, and candy canes in the open spaces.

3. Place the white chocolate chips, milk chocolate chips, nonpareils, and Sno-Caps in the ramekins. Place the crushed candy canes and shredded coconut in the bowls. Serve with whipped cream.

My Perfect Bite: Toasted-marshmallow hot cocoa, piled high with whipped cream and topped with mini marshmallows, crushed peppermint, and milk chocolate chips with a piece of dark chocolate peppermint bark to garnish.

Bottoms Up! Hot cocoa, obviously! You could always add some Kahlúa, Baileys, or even bourbon for a little kick.

MOVIE NIGHT BOARD

●○○ $$$

This board is full of my favorite movie theater treats, but switch up the ingredients to fit your family's preferences. I upped the nostalgia factor with a retro popcorn box I found online, but you can also use a large bowl. All that matters is that you have enough on your board to put you in a candy coma! *Serves 6 to 8*

Accessories: 3 small bowls, 1 retro popcorn box (optional)

Board: 15-inch round, wood with rim

1 (5-ounce) package Nerds gummy clusters or other gummy candy

1 (5-ounce) package malted milk balls

1 (3-ounce) package peanut M&M's

3 to 4 cups buttered popcorn

2 to 3 handfuls pretzels

1 (8-ounce) package gummy bears

1 (8-ounce) package mini peanut butter cups

1 (8-ounce) package mini KitKats

1 (8-ounce) package Sour Patch Kids

1 (5-ounce) package Mike and Ikes

1 (7-ounce) package red licorice

1. Place three small bowls on the board. Fill one with the gummy clusters, one with the malted milk balls, and the other with peanut M&M's.

2. Fill the popcorn box with the popcorn and place it on one side of the board, allowing some of the popcorn to spill out. Add more popcorn to fill out that section of the board.

3. Add the pretzels and remaining candy to the board in whatever pattern you think looks best. I recommend separating the chocolates with the rainbow candies, rather than having all the chocolates together, to achieve color variety across the board.

My Perfect Bite: An obnoxiously large handful of buttered popcorn followed up with as many Nerds Gummy Clusters as I can fit into my mouth at one time.

Bottoms Up! The round, creamy flavors of buttered popcorn pair beautifully with that bottle of oaked chardonnay you have sitting in your wine cabinet! Or even just an ice-cold Coke.

Make sure to select a board with high edges to avoid having candies fall off onto your couch. I taped the popcorn box to the edge so that it tipped onto the board. This creates the feeling of abundance and also ensures that the box doesn't take up too much surface area.

SO VERY FONDUE YOU

●●○ $$$

Perfect for Valentine's Day, Galentine's Day, or date night, this chocolate fondue board is the sweetest way to end your night. I found heart-shaped crackers and a cocotte to play up the romance, but you can use whatever you have on hand. *Serves 4 to 6*

Accessories: 1 ramekin, 1 small bowl

Board: 12-inch square, wood

Chocolate Fondue

6 ounces semisweet chocolate

4 ounces milk chocolate

⅓ cup whole milk

⅓ cup heavy cream

½ teaspoon pure vanilla extract

Fine sea salt

For the Board

⅓ cup cherry-cabernet jam or jam of choice

1 (5-ounce) wedge cranberry white Stilton

1 (7-ounce) package Neufchâtel

2 handfuls crackers

1 Genoa salami rose (page 194)

½ pound cake, cut into bite-size pieces

½ (16-ounce) package strawberries

2 bunches red grapes

1 (6-ounce) package raspberries

2 handfuls white chocolate–covered pretzels

1 to 2 handfuls pink-and-white nonpareils

1 to 2 handfuls Candied Nuts (page 145) or store-bought

Rosemary sprigs

Anything tastes good covered in chocolate! Try cakes, cookies, or marshmallows. Adding a few organic fresh roses to the board will crank up the romance, too!

1. **Make the Chocolate Fondue:** In a saucepan over low heat, combine the semisweet and milk chocolates, milk, and cream, stirring often so that mixture doesn't burn, until the chocolate melts. Stir in the vanilla and add salt to taste. Leave mixture in the pan over very low heat, stirring occasionally, until you're ready to serve.

2. **Assemble the board:** Place a ramekin and a small bowl on the board. Fill the ramekin with jam. Place the Stilton and Neufchâtel on opposite sides of the board.

3. Starting from the top of the board, begin to place the crackers, one on top of the other, until you reach the bottom. Add the salami rose.

4. If desired, create hearts from the pound cake and strawberries using a small cookie cutter before placing them on the board. Add the grapes, raspberries, pretzels, and nonparelis. Fill in the remaining space with the candied nuts. Garnish with rosemary.

5. Fill the bowl with the warm chocolate fondue just before serving. Leave the remaining fondue on the stove to keep warm and refill the board as needed.

My Perfect Bite: Hear me out on this one: a schmear of cranberry white Stilton on a cracker with a drizzle of chocolate fondue. You won't regret it!

Bottoms Up! Pop some bubbly! For extra flair, add some berries to the glass before topping up.

HO-HO-HOLIDAY COOKIES

●○○ $$$

Dessert is the best part of any holiday party . . . or is it the drinks? I could be swayed either way. You'll be sure to secure an invite to all the season's soirees with this board full of holiday cheer in hand. Fill it with your favorite holiday cookie recipes and seasonal sweets to make it more personal, or dress up store-bought treats. *Serves 8 to 10*

Board: 13-inch round, wood

1 small holiday rum cake

3 Gingerbread Cookies (page 162) or store-bought

5 raspberry linzer cookies

1 to 2 handfuls mini ginger babies or other mini holiday cookies

4 pizzelles

3 gingersnaps

6 sugar cookies

5 panettone slices

6 peppermint Milano cookies

Winter greens, such as holly leaves, cypress, or rosemary

Frosted Cranberries (page 169) or store-bought

1. At the the center of the board, place the rum cake. Create a layer of cookies, building outward from the center, with the gingerbread cookies, linzer cookies, and ginger babies.

2. Continuing to working outward, add the pizzelles, gingersnaps, sugar cookies, panettone, and peppermint cookies. Garnish with a few sprigs of winter greens and frosted cranberries

My Perfect Bite: Pizzelles have been my favorite holiday cookie since I can remember. My mom makes them every year! I'm filling up my plate with pizzelles and a couple of frosted cranberries.

Bottoms Up! Pour a glass of classic eggnog! The crunchy cookies with creamy eggnog is the perfect contrast.

HOLIDAY HAPPY HOUR

●○○ $$$

This board is sure to impress your guests during the holiday season. The spread of sweet and savory snacks pairs well with just about any cocktail. The key here is to splurge on the items that really make an impact, like cheeses and charcuterie, and save a few dollars on the ones that just offer a helping hand. *Serves 8*

Accessories: 2 ramekins

Board: 15-inch round, wood

½ (7-ounce) jar garlic-stuffed olives

1 (3-ounce) jar fig and honey jam

1 (8-ounce) wedge Gorgonzola

1 (6-ounce) wedge triple crème Brie

1 (6-ounce) round cranberry white cheddar

1 blood orange, sliced

3 bunches purple grapes

1 (6-ounce) box pistachio pomegranate crisps

6 ounces prosciutto slices

6 ounces Toscano salami slices

1 (6-ounce) package blackberries

1 cup Frosted Cranberries (page 169)
   or store-bought

1 (3-ounce) bar dark chocolate, broken into pieces

Rosemary sprigs

1. Place two ramekins on the board. Fill one with the olives and one with the jam.

2. Add the Gorgonzola, Brie, and cheddar cheeses across from each other on the board. Crumble the end of the Gorgonzola, if desired.

3. Layer the orange slices, one over the other, on opposite sides of the board. Add the grapes sporadically. Create a pile of crisps. Ribbon the prosciutto across the board. For step-by-step instructions, see page 193. Make a small pile of salami.

4. Fill in the remaining space with the blackberries, frosted cranberries, and dark chocolate pieces. Garnish with rosemary sprigs.

My Perfect Bite: Pistachio pomegranate crisp with some fig and honey jam, Gorgonzola crumbles, and a frosted cranberry.

Bottoms Up! Use an inexpensive bottle of merlot to make some Mulled Wine (page 181). It looks super fancy without all the fuss!

This board may look like a million bucks, but you can still wow on any budget by using snacks you have on hand. I always have grapes and chocolate in my pantry! The best thing about boards is that the options are endless!

HARRY & DAVID®
GIFT BASKET BOARD

●○○ $$$

One of the most delicious things about the holidays is the generous gift baskets friends and family bring when they visit. My favorite baskets to give and receive are from Harry & David because they're filled with specialty cheeses, charcuterie, artisan crackers, and fresh fruit—all of the ingredients you need for a stunning snack board. Here's some inspiration for how you can use a Harry & David gift basket—or any holiday gift basket—to make showstopping spreads for your family and friends to enjoy. *Serves 4 to 5*

Accessories: 1 ramekin, 1 medium bowl

Board: 13-inch round, wood

½ (10-ounce) jar sesame honey mustard dip

1 (10-ounce) jar pepper & onion relish

1 (4-ounce) block sharp white cheddar, sliced

1 (6-ounce) round Gouda

1 apple, sliced

2 pears, sliced

2 to 3 handfuls honey-wheat pretzels

2 to 3 handfuls three-seed crackers

6 ounces dry salami slices

2 to 3 handfuls mixed nuts

Lemon thyme sprigs

1. Place a ramekin and a medium bowl on the board. Fill the ramekin with the mustard dip and the bowl with the relish.

2. Layer the cheddar, placing one slice over the other, in a line across the board. Place the Gouda opposite of the cheddar, then cut a few wedges out. Fan out the apple and pear slices on opposite sides of the board.

3. Add the pretzels and crackers. Place the salami around the Gouda. Fill in the remaining space with the mixed nuts. Garnish with lemon thyme sprigs.

My Perfect Bite: An apple slice, sharp white cheddar, dry salami, and a small spoonful of mustard dip.

Bottoms Up! Enjoy this board with a Smoked Rosemary & Royal Riviera Pear Bourbon Spritzer (page 177). You can use the seasonal pears from your box or splurge for Harry & David's beloved Royal Riviera® pears.

FIG SPREAD
Original
FIG IS INSPECTED FOR QUALITY

great
taste
2020

SPRUCE · PINE ·

TREE FARM

cut & carry

THE GIFT OF HOLIDAY CHEER

●○○ $$$

Give the gift of cheese, charcuterie, and cheer this holiday season! Fill a decorative box or holiday tin with your favorite specialty cheeses and seasonal treats for a present that will warm the hearts and bellies of all your loved ones. See page 188 for tips and tricks on how to make your gift box travel ready. *Serves 4*

Board: 9.5-by-7 decorative box or tin

1 (5-ounce) round Boursin of choice

1 (6-ounce) wedge Cello Copper Kettle
  (hard cow's milk cheese), sliced

1 (2-ounce) jar jam or fruit spread of choice

1 (2-ounce) jar honey

6 to 8 flatbread crackers

8 ounces Italian dry salami slices

1 handful blackberries

1 to 2 handfuls maple pecan snack mix

1 (3-ounce) bar dark chocolate, broken into pieces

½ cup Frosted Cranberries (page 169)
  or store-bought

Frosted Rosemary (page 169)
  or fresh rosemary sprigs

Thyme sprigs

1. Place the Boursin and Copper Kettle cheeses in opposite corners of the box. Place the jars of jam and honey in the box.

2. Lean the crackers against the Boursin. Make two small piles of salami.

3. Add the blackberries, snack mix, and chocolate into any open spaces. Make a few small piles of the frosted cranberries. Garnish with frosted rosemary and thyme sprigs.

My Perfect Bite: A hefty scoop of shallot and chive Boursin on a sea salt cracker with a maple pecan and a drizzle of honey.

Bottoms Up! If you're feeling extra generous, gift a bottle of pinot blanc. This medium- to full-bodied wine offers flavors of apple, citrus, and white flower that will bring a nice freshness to the selection of decadent cheese.

FESTIVAL OF DE-LIGHTS

●●○ $$$

For a spread that sparkles as bright as the menorah during the Festival of Lights, you'll definitely want to serve up this Hanukkah board. Filled with blue, white, and gold goodies and the traditional fried foods that celebrate the season, it's the perfect way to turn your Hanukkah celebration into a family-friendly board everyone can munch on in between turns spinning the dreidel. *Serves 8 to 10*

Accessories: 3 small bowls or ramekins
Board: 20-by-15-inch rectangle, wood

⅓ cup apple sauce

⅓ cup sour cream

1 bunch scallions, sliced

1 loaf challah bread

6 potato latkes

3 sufganiyot (jelly donuts)

2 handfuls pita crackers

1 (6-ounce) package blueberries

1 (16-ounce) or 2 (8-ounce) rounds double crème Brie

1 (8-ounce) wedge Roquefort

1 (4-ounce) log wild blueberry, lemon, and thyme goat cheese, such as Vermont Creamery brand, or other blue-tinted cheese

6 blue-and-white sugar cookies

1 to 2 handfuls dark chocolate truffles, such as Lindt brand

1 to 2 handfuls chocolate-covered caramels, such as Rolo brand

1 to 2 handfuls blue Hershey's Kisses

Dill sprigs

1. Place three small bowls or ramekins on the board. Fill them with the apple sauce, sour cream, and scallions. Place the challah on a corner of the board, off to the side.

2. Layer the latkes, one on top of the other, on the board. In another corner of the board, stack the sufganiyot, being careful not to smudge the jelly.

3. Add the Brie, Roquefort, and goat cheese. Place a few piles of the pita crackers and blueberries around the board where space allows.

4. Fill in the remaining space with the sugar cookies, truffles, chocolate-covered caramels, and Kisses. Garnish with dill sprigs.

My Perfect Bite: A crispy latke topped with sour cream and a sprinkle of scallions, followed up with a big bite of sufganiyot.

Bottoms Up! Pair this feast with a Vanilla Old-Fashioned (page 172). The savory latkes paired with my sweet twist on a classic cocktail will round out your palate and highlight all the flavors on this board.

I used cookie cutters to create my shaped Brie for extra festiveness, but it will taste just as delicious no matter what it looks like. You could also use the reverse technique, where you remove the shape from the Brie and fill it with your favorite jam.

O CHRISTMAS CHEESE!

●●● $$$

On the naughty list this year? This spread of seasonal treats is sure you get you back on Santa's good side. To really get into the holiday spirit, I use a star-shaped cookie cutter to help top my tree. You could also use these ingredients to make a single cheese board in the shape of a tree, but I love the abundant display the three boards create. *Serves 10 to 12*

Accessories: 3 ramekins

Board: 16-by-7-, 11-by-7-, and 7-by-5-inch rectangles, wood

5 ounces Castelvetrano olives

½ (5-ounce) package honeycomb

½ pomegranate, plus ¼ cup pomegranate seeds

1 (4-ounce) round Little Hosmer (soft-ripened cow's milk cheese)

1 (6-ounce) wedge cranberry Wensleydale (fresh sheep's or cow's milk cheese)

1 (8-ounce) wedge Mimolette (hard cow's milk cheese), sliced

1 (8-ounce) wedge Humboldt Fog (soft-ripened goat's milk cheese)

1 to 2 handfuls rosemary and sea salt crackers

4 to 6 Parmesan crisps

1 to 2 handfuls gingerbread and spiced pear crackers or other seasonal crackers

6 ounces dark rum salami slices, folded into triangles

6 ounces soppressata slices, rolled

6 ounces bresaola slices

1 (6-ounce) package raspberries

1 (6-ounce) package blackberries

2 to 3 handfuls miniature holiday cookies

1 to 2 handfuls roasted macadamia nuts

2 to 3 cups Frosted Cranberries (page 169) or store-bought

1 cube sharp cheddar

Candy canes

Dried Citrus (page 166) or store-bought

Frosted Rosemary (page 169) or fresh rosemary sprigs

continued »

1. Lay out all three boards with the longest board placed horizontally at the bottom, the medium board in the middle, and the smallest board at the top. Place one ramekin at the top for the star.

2. Place one ramekin on the middle board and fill it with the olives. Place one ramekin on the bottom board and fill with the honeycomb. Add the ½ pomegranate to the middle board.

3. Place the Little Hosmer and Wensleydale on the bottom board. Fan out the slices of Mimolette on the middle board. Place the Humboldt Fog on the top board.

4. Layer in the sea salt crackers on the bottom board, Parmesan crisps on the middle board, and gingerbread crackers on the top board.

5. Add the salami to the bottom and top boards. Make a small pile of rolled soppressata on the bottom board. Create a ribbon of bresaola around the ramekin of olives on the middle board. For step-by-step directions see page 193.

6. Add the raspberries, blackberries, miniature cookies, and nuts sporadically across all three boards. Fill the ramekin at the top with the cranberries and place the cheddar "star" on top. Divide the remaining cranberries among the boards.

7. Fill in remaining space with candy canes, dried citrus, and pomegranate seeds. Garnish with frosted rosemary.

My Perfect Bite: A piece of beautiful Mimolette with bresaola, honeycomb, and a sprinkle of pomegranate seeds.

Bottoms Up! I'm definitely sipping on some Mulled Wine (page 181). This warm spiced drink is the perfect pairing for the cheeses on this board.

GATHER ROUND GRAZING TABLE

● ● ● $$$

Behold! The only answer you'll need to "What should we serve?" at any gathering. A table full of seasonal fruit, spiced treats, and all the specialty cheese you could imagine. The best part is, once the board is prepped and ready to enjoy, the stress of hosting dissapears and you slide right into being able to enjoy the party . . . and a few glasses of wine! I used a very large 40-by-15-inch board for this, but you can use anything that will protect your table. Check out some suggestions on page 4.
Serves 15 to 20

Accessories: 2 ramekins, 1 medium bowl, 3 small bowls

Board: 40-by-15-inch rectangle, wood

1 (10-ounce) jar spiced pumpkin spread

1 wedge Humboldt Fog (soft-ripened goat's milk cheese)

1 wedge aged Gouda

1 wedge cinnamon Toscano or cinnamon-dusted cheddar Parmesan

1 (8-ounce) wedge Parmigiano-Reggiano

2 (4-ounce) logs cranberry-cinnamon goat cheese, such as Celebrity brand

1 (8-ounce) round double crème Brie

2 pounds grapes, assorted varieties

1 (6-ounce) package gingerbread and spiced pear crackers

1 (4-ounce) package sourdough flatbread bites

1 (12-ounce) box maple leaf cookies

1 loaf zucchini bread

1 recipe Apple and Butternut Squash Bruschetta (page 154)

8 ounces soppressata slices

8 ounces prosciutto slices

8 ounces Chianti salami slices

8 ounces Genoa salami slices

1 (12-ounce) package blackberries

1 (12-ounce) package raspberries

1 (6-ounce) package golden berries or dried apricots

4 fresh figs, halved

2 cups Candied Nuts (page 145), or store-bought

1 pound Frosted Cranberries (page 169) or store-bought

1 (6-ounce) jar Manzanilla olives

1 (8-ounce) can macadamia nuts

⅓ cup honey

Frosted Rosemary (page 169) or fresh rosemary sprigs

continued »

1. Place the two ramekins, one medium bowl, three small bowls, and jar of pumpkin spread evenly along the length of the table, making sure there is space between each item.

2. Following a similar pattern, place the Humboldt Fog, Gouda, Toscano, Parmigiano-Reggiano, goat cheese, and Brie along the board.

3. Add the grapes, wrapping them around bowls and ramekins or placing them on the edge of the board. Add small piles or lines of crunchy items, including the crackers, flatbread bites, cookies, zucchini bread, and bruschetta. (I'd suggest assembling a few pieces of bruschetta to demonstrate how they should be enjoyed.)

4. Place the sopressata, prosciutto, chianti salami, and genoa salami evenly along the board.

5. Fill open spaces with blackberries, raspberries, golden berries, figs, and candied pecans.

6. Fill in the empty bowls and ramekins with frosted cranberries, Manzanilla olives, macadamia nuts, and honey. Garnish with frosted rosemary.

My Perfect Bite: This spread needs a plate! A slice each of Humboldt Fog and goat cheese, a few spiced crackers, some soppressata, frosted cranberries, and grapes, a handful of candied pecans, and a spoonful of spiced pumpkin spread.

Bottoms Up! A well-balanced pinot noir with delightfully smooth aromas of red plum, currant, and anise.

Use different folding techniques, like rolling, ribboning, slicing, etc., for the charcuterie to create a variety of textures and height on the board. Experiment with different ways to slice and dice your cheeses, too. See pages 189–194 of the Hopeless Hostess Appendix for more ideas.

RING IN THE NEW YEAR

●●○　　　$$$

What pairs perfectly with Champagne and a night of dancing around in a party hat? Cheese! Ring in the new year with this board that is sure to turn any New Year's party into a black-tie affair. *Serves 6 to 8*

Accessories: 1 ramekin, 1 small bowl, 2 caviar serving dishes, 2 caviar spoons

Board: 20-by-12-inch rectangle, slate

4 ounces crème fraîche

1 (3-ounce) jar fig spread

Ice cubes

1 (1.75-ounce) jar salmon roe

1 (1.75-ounce) jar black tobiko roe

5 to 6 pieces edible gold leaf

1 (8-ounce) round Nettle Meadow Kunik (soft-ripened cow's and goat's milk cheese)

1 (8-ounce) wedge Alp Blossom Swiss, sliced

1 (8-ounce) wedge Humboldt Fog (soft-ripened goat's milk cheese)

10 ounces peppered salami slices, folded in half

1 (4.5-ounce) package cocktail blinis

1 or 2 handfuls olive oil crostini or crackers

1 handful gorgonzola-stuffed olives

1 (6-ounce) package blackberries

1 (6-ounce) package blueberries

1 to 2 handfuls Ferrero Rocher hazelnut chocolates

1 handful Prosecco gummy bears or other festive candy

Rosemary sprigs

Thyme sprigs

1. Place one ramekin and one small bowl on the board. Fill the bowl with the crème fraîche and the ramekin with the fig spread.

2. Place the caviar serving dishes in opposite corners of the board. Fill the bottom of each dish with ice. Fill the top bowls with the caviar. Gently set on top of the ice to chill.

3. Delicately place the gold leaf sheets on top of the Kunik, covering the top entirely. Place the Kunik on the board, followed by the Swiss and Humboldt Fog.

4. Create a ribbon across the board with the salami. For step-by-step instructions, see page 193.

5. Place the cocktail blinis around the caviar serving dishes. Add the crostini in any open space on either side of the board.

6. In the remaining space, add the blackberries, blueberries, olives, chocolates, and gummy bears. Garnish with rosemary and thyme.

My Perfect Bite: Gold-crusted wedge of Kunik, fig spread, and a blackberry.

Bottoms Up! Now's the time to pop that bottle of Champagne you've been saving!

Edible gold leaf brings instant glitz and glamour to your board! You can find it pretty inexpensively online, but be sure to purchase quality gold leaf. Cheaper versions can include impurities.

Put down the silver spoon for the caviar! The metal will transfer a bitter, metallic taste to your very delicate caviar.

6
DIPS,
SNACKS,
COCKTAILS
& MORE

HERBY VEGETABLE DIP

Pairs well with: Classy Crudité (page 28), Game Day Board (page 98) *Makes 1½ cups*

1 cup mayonnaise

½ cup sour cream

1 tablespoon dried parsley

1 tablespoon dried chives

1 tablespoon dried minced garlic

1 teaspoon dried tarragon

1 teaspoon dried dill

½ teaspoon garlic powder

½ teaspoon onion powder

¼ teaspoon paprika

Fine sea salt

Freshly ground black pepper

1. In a medium bowl, whisk together the mayo, sour cream, parsley, chives, minced garlic, tarragon, dill, garlic powder, onion powder, and paprika. Season with salt and pepper to taste.

2. For best taste, transfer to an airtight container and refrigerate for at least 3 hours before serving. Store in the refrigerator for up to 1 week.

PESTO

Pairs well with: Burrata & Heirloom Tomato Salad (page 59, Build-a-Bagel Board (page 110), Say "Cheez" (vegan version) (page 46) *Makes 1 cup*

2 cups packed fresh basil leaves

3 garlic cloves

¼ cup pine nuts

½ cup freshly grated Parmesan

½ cup freshly grated Pecorino Romano

Fine sea salt

Freshly ground black pepper

½ to ¾ cup extra-virgin olive oil

1. Combine the basil, garlic, pine nuts, Parmesan, and Pecorino Romano in a food processor. Season with salt and pepper to taste. With the food processor running, add the olive oil in a slow stream until the sauce is emulsified. Start with ½ cup and add more until you achieve your desired consistency.

2. Store in an airtight container in the refrigerator for up to 1 week.

Pesto is so easy to transform! It's usually made with pine nuts, but other nuts, including walnuts, almonds, and cashews, can be used to give a different flavor profile. You can also use different greens, like arugula or kale, and other hard cheeses. I like to include both Parmesan and Pecorino Romano for an extra hit of salty cheesiness. You can even make vegan pesto—just substitute 3 to 4 tablespoons of nutritional yeast for the cheeses.

Herby Vegetable Dip
(page 138)

Pesto (page 138)

Creamy Hummus
(page 140)

CREAMY HUMMUS

Pairs well with: Say "Cheez" (page 46), Taste of the Mediterranean (page 35), Classy Crudité (page 28) *Makes 2 cups*

Juice of 1 lemon, plus more as needed

2 garlic cloves

½ teaspoon fine sea salt, plus more as needed

½ cup tahini

2 to 4 tablespoons water, or as needed

1½ cups cooked chickpeas, drained and rinsed

½ teaspoon ground cumin

2 tablespoons extra-virgin olive oil

Pinch Paprika (optional)

1 handful Crispy Chickpeas (page 144) or store-bought (optional)

1. In a food processor, combine the lemon juice, garlic, and salt. Chop until the garlic is nearly minced, then let the mixture rest for 5 to 10 minutes to allow the garlic flavor to mellow out.

2. Add the tahini to the mixture and process until thick and creamy. With the food processor running, drizzle in 2 tablespoons of water and continue to blend until the mixture is super smooth and creamy.

3. Add the chickpeas and cumin. With the food processor running, drizzle in the olive oil and blend until the mixture is super smooth. If the mixture is still too thick, add water, 1 tablespoon at a time, until you reach your desired consistency.

4. Taste and adjust the seasoning as necessary. Add another pinch of salt and/or a squeeze of lemon juice if you need a bit more flavor.

5. Serve in a bowl garnished with a pinch of paprika and a handful of crispy chickpeas, if desired.

6. Store in an airtight container in the refrigerator for up to 1 week.

ELOTE DIP

Pairs well with: Ultimate Taco Tuesday (page 67), The Grill Master (page 64), Fun in the Sun (page 60) *Makes 5 cups*

4 cups fresh or frozen corn kernels

1 tablespoon salted butter

1 jalapeño, seeded and diced

Pinch of salt

3 tablespoons mayonnaise

⅓ cup Cotija cheese

1 garlic clove, minced

1 teaspoon chili powder, plus more for garnish

1 teaspoon onion powder

2 limes, 1 juiced, and one cut into wedges, for serving

½ teaspoon grated lime zest

⅓ cup chopped fresh cilantro, plus more for garnish

1. In a medium skillet over medium heat, melt the butter. Add the corn kernels, jalapeño, and a pinch of salt. Reduce heat to medium-low and cook for 8 to 10 minutes, stirring occasionally.

2. In a medium bowl, place the corn mixture. Add the mayonnaise, Cotija cheese, garlic, chili powder, onion powder, lime zest and juice, and cilantro.

3. Garnish with a pinch of chili powder, more cilantro, and a lime wedge.

4. Store in an airtight container in the refrigerator for up to 3 days.

Savory Spiced Nuts
(page 143)

Candied Bacon
(page 143)

Crispy Chickpeas
(page 144)

Candied Nuts
(page 145)

SAVORY SPICED NUTS

Pairs well with: Spice, Spice, Baby (page 93), Oktoberfest (page 102), The Grill Master (page 64) *Makes 1 pound (about 4 cups)*

1 pound mixed nuts or nuts of choice, such as pecans, almonds, and/or cashews

2 tablespoons extra-virgin olive oil

1 teaspoon chili powder

1 teaspoon garlic powder

1 teaspoon onion powder

1 teaspoon ground cumin

½ teaspoon freshly ground black pepper

½ teaspoon fine sea salt

¼ teaspoon ground cayenne pepper

1. Preheat the oven to 350°F. Line a large rimmed baking sheet with parchment paper or aluminum foil.

2. Combine the nuts and olive oil in a medium bowl, tossing to coat completely. Add the chili powder, garlic powder, onion powder, cumin, black pepper, salt, and cayenne pepper and toss to coat again.

3. Place the seasoned nuts in single layer on the prepared baking sheet and roast, stirring halfway through, for 15 minutes, until toasted and darker in color.

4. Remove the nuts the from oven and allow them to cool. Store in an airtight container at room temperature for up to 2 weeks.

CANDIED BACON

Pairs well with: Brimful Brunch (page 38), Spice, Spice, Baby (page 93), Build-Your-Own Bloody Mary (page 32) *Makes about 12 slices*

1 pound thick-cut bacon slices

½ cup light brown sugar

½ tablespoon red pepper flakes

½ teaspoon freshly ground black pepper

½ teaspoon fine sea salt

¼ teaspoon ground cayenne pepper

You can leave your bacon whole or chop it up into bite-size pieces.

1. Preheat the oven to 375°F.

2. Line a large rimmed baking sheet with parchment paper or aluminum foil. Place the bacon slices on the prepared baking sheet.

3. In a small bowl, combine the brown sugar, red pepper flakes, black pepper, salt, and cayenne pepper. Sprinkle the sugar mixture over the bacon slices, fully coating all of the slices.

4. Bake for 30 minutes, or until the bacon is brown and crispy. Remove from the oven and let cool for 10 minutes. Carefully transfer the bacon to a cooling rack and let cool for another 10 minutes. Refrigerate in an airtight container for up to 5 days.

CRISPY CHICKPEAS

Pairs well with: Taste of the Mediterranean (page 35), Classy Crudité (page 28), Holiday Happy Hour (page 121) *Makes 1½ cups*

1½ cups cooked chickpeas, drained and rinsed

3 tablespoons extra-virgin olive oil

1 teaspoon fine sea salt

Paprika, ground cumin, Italian seasoning, or other spices (optional)

1. Preheat the oven to 425°F and line a large rimmed baking sheet with parchment paper.

2. Dry the chickpeas well using a kitchen towel or paper towels. Pat them dry and remove any loose skins.

3. Transfer the chickpeas to the baking sheet and toss them with the olive oil and salt. Spread them evenly across the baking sheet in a single layer.

4. Roast for 25 to 30 minutes, or until golden brown and crisp. If the chickpeas aren't crispy enough, keep roasting until they are! Store in an airtight container at room temperature and enjoy within 2 to 3 days.

Feel free to add your favorite seasonings to spice these up! A combo I would recommend is 1½ teaspoons chili powder, 1 teaspoon cumin, ½ teaspoon paprika, 1 teaspoon black pepper, and a pinch of sea salt. There are tons of other seasoning combinations, too. Experiment until you find your favorite flavor!

CANDIED NUTS

Pairs well with: Fall Harvest (page 85), Gather Round Grazing Table (page 131), So Very Fondue You Board (page 117)
Makes 1 pound (about 4 cups)

2 egg whites

1 stick salted butter

1½ cups granulated sugar

1 pound nuts of choice, such as pecans, almonds, and/or cashews

1. Preheat the oven to 350°F.

2. In a medium bowl, using an electric mixer on medium speed, beat the egg whites for 5 to 7 minutes, or until stiff peaks form.

3. Place the butter on a large rimmed baking sheet and melt it in the oven, about 4 minutes. Watch closely so that the butter doesn't burn!

4. While the butter is melting, use a spatula to fold the sugar into the egg whites until thoroughly combined. Add the nuts to the mixture and stir, coating all the nuts completely.

5. Pour the nut mixture onto the baking sheet and combine with the melted butter. Spread the nuts evenly across the baking sheet in single layer. Bake for 30 minutes, stirring and flipping the nuts every 10 minutes, until brown and crunchy.

6. Remove the nuts from oven and allow them to cool. Store in an airtight container at room temperature and enjoy within 1 week.

QUICK PICKLED RED ONIONS

Pairs well with: Towering Tea Party (page 42), Build-a-Bagel Board (page 110), Ultimate Taco Tuesday (page 67) *Makes ½ cup*

3 cups water

¾ cup white vinegar

½ teaspoon granulated sugar

½ teaspoon fine sea salt

1 garlic clove, lightly crushed

6 whole black peppercorns

2 thyme sprigs, broken in half

1 small red onion, thinly sliced

1. In a small pot over high heat, bring the water to a boil.

2. In a small jar with a lid, shake or stir together the vinegar, sugar, salt, garlic, peppercorns, and thyme. Add the onions to the jar.

3. Carefully pour the water into the jar, making sure the onions are fully submerged. Tightly close the lid and gently shake to distribute the flavorings.

4. Refrigerate for at least 1 hour before serving. (You will notice the color change.) Store for up to 3 weeks in the refrigerator.

Try adding a few Sichuan peppercorns into the mix if you like the mouth-numbing sensation like me!

WATERMELON, FETA & MINT SALAD

Pairs well with: Melon Ball Salad Platter (page 56), Burrata & Heirloom Tomato Salad (page 59), The Grill Master (page 64) *Serves 4*

3 tablespoons extra-virgin olive oil

4 teaspoons red wine vinegar

½ teaspoon fine sea salt

6 cups cubed seedless watermelon

4 ounces feta, crumbled

¼ red onion, thinly sliced

¼ cup Candied Nuts (page 145), or store-bought, chopped (optional)

3 tablespoons coarsely chopped fresh mint

Fresh mint leaves

Flaky sea salt

1. In a small bowl, whisk together the olive oil, vinegar, and fine sea salt.

2. On a large round board with a rim or in a large bowl, combine the watermelon, feta, onion, candied pecans, if using, and chopped mint. Drizzle on the dressing and toss to combine. Garnish with mint leaves and flaky sea salt.

SPICY FRIED GOAT CHEESE BALLS

Pairs well with: Game Day Board (page 98), Spice, Spice, Baby (page 93), Holiday Happy Hour (page 121)

½ cup all-purpose flour

1 cup panko bread crumbs

2 large eggs

1 (8-ounce) log goat cheese

3 tablespoons hot honey, plus more for drizzling

1 teaspoon red pepper flakes

Vegetable oil

Flaky sea salt

If you can't find hot honey, substitute with regular honey for a sweeter goat cheese ball and enjoy with a sprinkle of coarse sugar on top. You can also make your own hot honey using my Hopeless Hostess tip on page 93.

1. Put the flour and bread crumbs into separate small bowls. Beat the eggs in another small bowl. In a medium bowl, combine the goat cheese, honey, and red pepper flakes.

2. Take 1 heaping tablespoon of the cheese mixture and roll it into a ball. Roll the ball in the flour, coating evenly. Then place the ball in the eggs, making sure it's completely covered. Then roll the ball in the bread crumbs, until evenly coated. Resubmerge the ball in the eggs and toss in the bread crumbs again. Place on a plate. Repeat this process with the remaining cheese mixture.

3. In a shallow pan, heat about 1 inch of vegetable oil, or enough to submerge half the cheese balls, to 375°F to 400°F. The oil should be hot enough that a crumb of panko simmers when you drop it in.

4. Working in batches, place the cheese balls into the oil and cook for 20 to 30 seconds, until browned on one side, then flip and repeat on the other side. Alternatively, you can air fry these at 400°F for 6 to 8 minutes, until browned and crispy.

5. Carefully lift out the fried cheese balls and transfer them to a paper towel–lined plate to drain. Sprinkle with flaky sea salt and serve with a drizzle of hot honey.

LAVENDER & PEACH CROSTINI

Pairs well with: Towering Tea Party (page 42), Spring Floral (page 53), Easter Sunday (page 50) *Serves 4*

1 (5-ounce) package honey-lavender goat cheese, such as Nettle Meadow brand

1 loaf ciabatta bread, sliced and toasted or grilled

Fine sea salt

3 yellow peaches, sliced

Wildflower honey

Thyme sprigs

Edible flowers (optional)

1. Spread the goat cheese over the toasty bread so that it gets melty and spreads evenly. Top with a pinch of salt and the peach slices.

2. Drizzle the crostini with the honey and garnish with thyme sprigs. Add edible flowers, if using.

Can't find honey-lavender goat cheese? Make your own! Take goat cheese, honey, and culinary lavender and whip together in a food processor.

APPLE & BUTTERNUT SQUASH BRUSCHETTA WITH HONEY RICOTTA & GARLIC TOASTS

Pairs well with: Gather Round Grazing Table (page 131), Thanksgiving Leftovers (page 105), Fall Harvest (page 85)
Serves 8 to 10

Apple & Butternut Squash Bruschetta

- 2 cups diced butternut squash
- 1 cup diced Granny Smith apples
- 2 tablespoons extra-virgin olive oil
- 1 teaspoon ground cinnamon
- 1 teaspoon ground nutmeg
- ½ teaspoon allspice
- ½ teaspoon ground cloves
- 1 teaspoon flaky sea salt
- 2 tablespoons fresh rosemary leaves

Honey Ricotta

- 1 cup ricotta cheese
- 3 tablespoons honey
- Fine sea salt
- Freshly ground black pepper

Garlic Toasts

- 1 French baguette, sliced into 8 to 10 pieces
- Extra-virgin olive oil
- Fine sea salt
- Freshly ground black pepper
- 2 garlic cloves
- 2 tablespoons balsamic glaze, for serving

1. Preheat the oven to 425°F. Line two baking sheets with parchment paper.

2. **Make the Apple & Butternut Squash Bruschetta:** In a large bowl, toss the squash and apples with the olive oil, cinnamon, nutmeg, allspice, cloves, sea salt, and rosemary. Spread evenly onto one prepared baking sheet and bake for 15 minutes, or until the squash and apples are tender. Remove and set aside to cool, leaving the oven on.

3. **Make the Honey Ricotta:** Meanwhile, in a medium bowl, combine the ricotta and honey. Season with salt and pepper to taste.

4. **Make the Garlic Toasts**: Meanwhile, brush the bread slices with olive oil and lightly sprinkle with salt and pepper on both sides. Place on the second prepared baking sheet in a single layer. Once the squash and apples are done, bake the bread for 4 to 5 minutes, or until golden brown and toasted. Remove from the oven, then gently rub the garlic cloves on the warm bread.

5. **Assemble the dish:** Spread about 1 tablespoon of the ricotta mixture onto each toast and top with the squash and apple mixture. Drizzle with the balsamic glaze before serving.

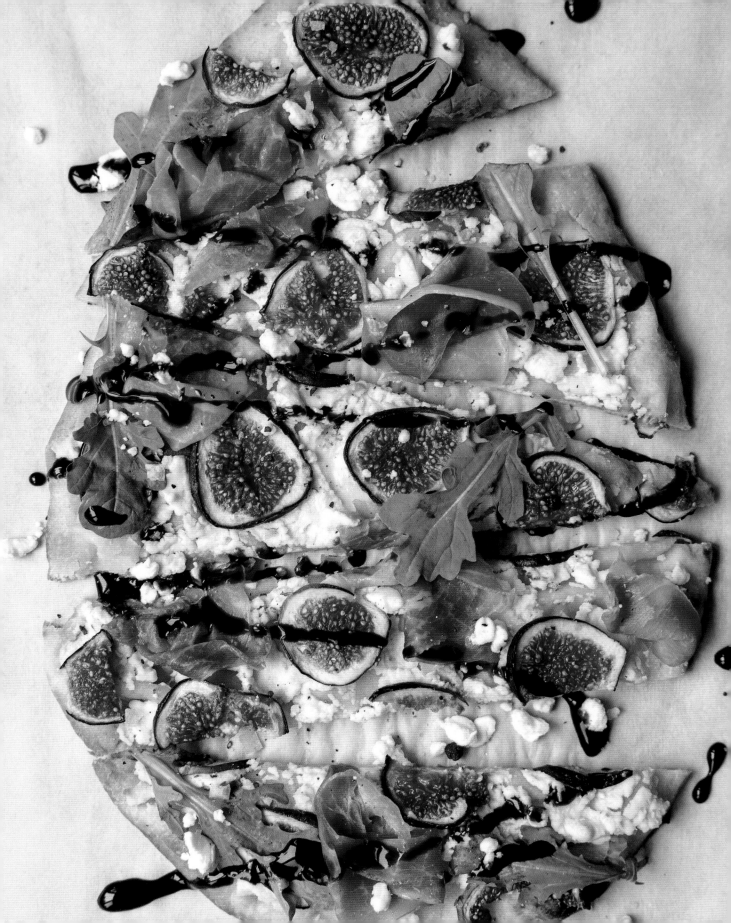

FIG, PROSCIUTTO & GOAT CHEESE FLATBREADS

Pairs well with: Fall Harvest (page 85, Holiday Happy Hour (page 121), C'est Charcuterie (page 41) *Serves 2*

2 (8-ounce) artisan flatbreads

2 tablespoons extra-virgin olive oil

Fine sea salt

Freshly ground black pepper

8 ounces honey goat cheese

6 fresh figs, thinly sliced

1 cup packed baby arugula

8 ounces prosciutto slices

Balsamic glaze, for serving

1. Preheat the oven to 450°F. Line a baking sheet with parchment paper.

2. Place the flatbreads on the baking sheet. Brush them with the olive oil and sprinkle with salt and pepper.

3. Crumble almost all of the goat cheese evenly over the flatbreads, reserving the rest. Bake for 3 to 4 minutes, or until the goat cheese has softened.

4. Using a knife, spread the goat cheese evenly across the flatbread. Top with the sliced figs and return to the oven for 12 to 15 minutes, until golden brown and crispy.

5. Top with the arugula and prosciutto. Sprinkle the reserved goat cheese over the flatbreads. Drizzle generously with balsamic glaze before serving

The topping combos are endless for this one! Try crumbled blue cheese, caramelized onions, and fresh arugula. Or keep it light with fresh kale, Creamy Hummus (page 140), and shaved Parmesan. I love to reach into the fridge and see what I can create with what I have on hand. A great use for those leftovers.

CRACKER-CRUSTED BAKED MAC & BRIE

Pairs well with: Gather Round Grazing Table (page 131), Ring in the New Year (page 134), Game Day Board (page 98) *Serves 2 to 4*

Cracker Crust

1 sleeve buttery crackers, such as Ritz brand, crushed

2 tablespoons salted butter, melted

Mac & Brie

2 (8-ounce) rounds double crème Brie

1 cup finely grated Parmesan

1 cup finely grated Grand Cru or other Alpine cheese

3 tablespoons unsalted butter, divided

3 tablespoons all-purpose flour

1½ cups milk, plus more as needed

½ teaspoon Dijon mustard

1 teaspoon garlic powder

Fine sea salt

Freshly ground black pepper

8 ounces pasta, cooked just under al dente

Dried parsley, for garnish

1. Preheat the oven to 375°F. Line a rimmed baking sheet with parchment paper.

2. **Make the Cracker Crust:** In a small bowl, mix together the crushed crackers and butter. Set aside.

3. **Make the Mac & Brie:** Straight out of the fridge, use a paring knife to cut circles out of the center of the Brie rounds. Leave about 1 centimeter around each round's edge to hold its shape. Scoop out the center of the Brie and place it in a large bowl. Return the rinds to the fridge. Add the Parmesan and Grand Cru to the Brie and mix to combine.

4. Melt the butter in a medium pot over medium heat. Add the flour and mix until combined. Cook the mixture, stirring constantly, for 2 to 3 minutes. (This is important to cook out the raw-flour taste.)

5. Add the milk, mustard, and garlic powder and keep cooking and stirring for 4 to 5 minutes, or until the sauce starts to thicken. Add the cheese mixture and stir until completely melted. Season with salt and pepper to taste. If the sauce is too thick, add milk, ¼ cup at a time, until the desired conistency is achieved.

6. Add the cooked pasta to the pot and toss with the sauce until well coated.

7. Place the reserved Brie rounds on the prepared baking sheet. Spoon the pasta mixture into each of the centers, top with about half of the cracker crust, and bake for 8 to 10 minutes, until the crackers are browned. Garnish with parsley to serve.

8. Pour the remaining pasta mixture into an ovenproof dish, top with the remaining cracker crust, and bake for 10 to 15 minutes. You'll use this to refill the Brie throughout the gathering.

You can cook your pasta while you preheat
the oven and make the cracker crust.

MINI CHERRY & BRIE GALETTES

Pairs well with: Red, White & Berries (page 75), Fall Harvest (page 85), Brimful Brunch (page 38) *Makes 4*

1 cup fresh cherries, pitted and thinly sliced

2 tablespoon raw sugar, plus more for sprinkling

1 sheet frozen puff pastry, thawed according to package instructions

4 tablespoons cherry preserves

½ (8-ounce) round triple crème Brie, cut into thin slices

1 large egg, beaten

Thyme sprigs

1. Preheat the oven to 425°F. Line a baking sheet with parchment paper.

2. In a medium bowl, combine the cherries and sugar.

3. Cut the puff pastry into four squares and place on the prepared baking sheet. Spread 1 tablespoon of preserves onto each square, making sure to leave a ¼-inch border.

4. Place two slices of Brie on each square and top with the sugared cherry slices. Press the cherries to lightly adhere them. Fold in the edges of the pastry to enclose the Brie and preserves. The cheese will spread, so make sure that you have a large enough border and that the edges are tucked in.

5. Lightly brush the edges of the pastry with the beaten egg and sprinkle with sugar. Bake for 12 to 15 minutes, or until the edges of the pastry are golden and crisp.

GINGERBREAD COOKIES

Pairs well with: Ho-Ho-Holiday Cookies (page 118), O Christmas Cheese! (page 129), Cozy Hot Cocoa Board (page 113)
Makes 30 cookies

Gingerbread Cookies

1½ sticks unsalted butter, softened

¾ cup packed light brown sugar

1 large egg

½ cup molasses

1½ teaspoons pure vanilla extract

3¼ cups all-purpose flour, plus more as needed

1 tablespoon ground cinnamon

1 tablespoon ground ginger

1 teaspoon baking soda

¾ teaspoon ground cloves

½ teaspoon fine sea salt

½ teaspoon ground nutmeg

Icing

2 cups powdered sugar, plus more as needed

3 to 4 tablespoons heavy cream, plus more as needed

½ teaspoon pure vanilla extract

1. **Make the Gingerbread Cookies:** In a large bowl using an electric hand mixer, beat the butter and brown sugar until fluffy, about 2 minutes. Add the egg, molasses, and vanilla and beat until combined.

2. In a separate large bowl, whisk together the flour, cinnamon, ginger, baking soda, cloves, salt, and nutmeg.

3. With the mixer on low speed, gradually add the flour mixture to the wet ingredients and mix until just combined. Be sure not to overmix!

4. Divide the dough into two equal portions and form them into 1-inch-thick discs. (They should be flattened, not round). Wrap the discs tightly in plastic wrap and refrigerate for 1 to 2 hours, or until the dough is chilled yet pliable.

5. Preheat the oven to 350°F and line two baking sheets with parchment paper.

6. Place one disc of dough on a lightly floured surface and use a floured rolling pin to roll the dough until it's about ¼ inch thick. Use cookie cutters (or even drinking glasses) to cut shapes out of the dough. Place the cookies on the prepared baking sheets.

7. Bake for 8 to 10 minutes, or until the edges of the cookies are crisp. Let cool for 5 minutes, then transfer them to a wire rack to finish cooling.

8. **Make the Icing:** When the cookies are cool, in a medium bowl, whisk together the powdered sugar, cream, and vanilla until smooth. If the icing is too thin, add in a little more powdered sugar. If the icing is too thick, add in a tiny bit of cream. You want a thicker consistency to ensure the icing stays in place and doesn't run on the cookie.

9. Transfer the icing to a resealable plastic bag (or a piping bag, if you have one). Snip the corner off the plastic and pipe the icing onto the cookies. Let the icing set until dry.

CHEESE "CAKE"

Pairs well with: Ring in the New Year
(page 134), Holiday Happy Hour (page 121),
Gather Round Grazing Table (page 131)
Serves 30 to 40

1 (5½-pound) round cranberry Wensleydale
(fresh sheep's or cow's milk cheese)

1 (2½-pound) round Queijo de Ovelha
Curado (semihard sheep's milk cheese)

1 (9-ounce) round Harbison (soft-ripened
cow's milk cheese)

1 (8-ounce) round Nettle Meadow Kunik (soft-
ripened cow's and goat's milk cheese)

1 (4-ounce) round Brie

Edible flowers, nuts, Dried Citrus (page 166),
and/or fresh herbs, for decorating

Honey, for "glue"

1. Place the Wensleydale onto a board, platter,
   or cake stand. Placing one on top of the
   other, gently add the Herdade da Maia,
   followed by the Harbison, Kunik, and Brie.

2. Decorate the cake with your chosen
   garnishes, starting with the bottom layer and
   working upward. Do not use the honey to
   adhere them at this point, wait until you have
   everything where you want it.

3. Once everything is in place, begin to adhere
   your decorations using the honey, starting
   from the bottom and working your way to
   the top.

4. If you're preparing this well before your
   event, store it in the fridge until about 1 hour
   before you're ready to serve. This will keep
   the cheese moist. Allow it to come to room
   temperature (the optimal temperature to eat
   cheese) before serving. If you plan to leave
   it in the fridge overnight, wrap it as carefully
   as possible to avoid dislocating any of the
   garnish.

Choose at least 4 to 5 cheeses to give the tower ample height and
achieve that "wow!" factor. Incorporate a variety of cheeses, like cow's
milk, sheep's milk, and goat's milk, as well as different textures, to
provide an array of choices. The cheese rounds will need to be able to
withstand the weight placed on top of them, so place the larger, harder
cheeses on the bottom and the smaller, softer cheeses at the top.

DRIED CITRUS

Pairs well with: C'est Charcuterie (page 41), The Gift of Holiday Cheer (page 125), Thankful for Desserts (page 106)

2 navel oranges, cut into ¼-inch slices

2 blood oranges, cut into ¼-inch slices

2 lemons, cut into ¼-inch slices

2 limes, cut into ¼-inch slices

1. Preheat the oven to 200°F (or 170°F if your oven can go even lower). Line a baking sheet with parchment paper.

2. Place the citrus slices in a single layer on the prepared baking sheet, making sure there is no overlapping. Bake for 3 to 6 hours, flipping every 2 hours, until the citrus has no more moisture and is brittle to the touch.

3. Remove from the oven and let cool completely. This will happen at different times for each fruit, so be sure to pay close attention. Store in an airtight container in the refrigerator for up to 1 year.

FROSTED ROSEMARY & FROSTED CRANBERRIES

Pairs well with: O Christmas Cheese!
(page 129), The Gift of Holiday Cheer (page
125), Holiday Happy Hour (page 121)
Makes 2 cups cranberries
Makes 4 to 5 rosemary sprigs

1 cup water

1 cup granulated sugar, plus more for coating

4 to 5 rosemary sprigs

1 (12-ounce) bag fresh cranberries,
  rinsed and picked through

*Reserve the infused simple syrup
and use for holiday cocktails!*

1. Line a rimmed baking sheet with parchment paper and place a cooling rack on top.

2. **For the Frosted Rosemary:** In a medium saucepan over medium-low heat, heat the water and sugar until the sugar is completely dissolved. Add the rosemary sprigs and let them soak for 2 to 3 minutes, then remove from the heat. Using tongs or a slotted spoon, transfer the rosemary to the cooling rack. Let sit overnight or for at least 4 hours, until sticky but not wet. Roll the rosemary in sugar until fully coated. Let dry until hardened, about 6 hours.

3. **For the Frosted Cranberries:** Add the cranberries to the sugar mixture and continue to cook, still over medium-low heat, for 5 to 7 minutes, or until the cranberries begin to split. With a slotted spoon, transfer the cranberries to the cooling rack. Let sit overnight or for at least 4 hours, until sticky but not wet. Roll the cranberries in sugar until fully coated. Let dry until hardened, about 6 hours. The fresher the cranberries, the longer they'll last.

4. Store in an airtight container at room temperature for 3 to 4 days. If after a few days you notice that the sugar is beginning to dissolve, give a second toss in sugar before serving.

ELDERFLOWER GIN SOUR

Pairs well with: Spring Floral (page 53),
So Very Fondue You (page 117), Burrata &
Heirloom Tomato Salad (page 59)
Makes 2 cocktails

3 ounces gin of choice

1 ounce St. Germain (elderflower liqueur)

1 egg white

1 ounce simple syrup, or to taste

Juice of ½ lemon

2 lemon twists (optional)

1. Combine the gin, St. Germain, egg white, simple syrup, and lemon juice in a cocktail shaker or large jar with a lid. Shake well.

2. Add enough ice to fill the shaker and shake again until you see a noticeable amount of foam in the shaker, about 1 minute. Strain into a glass and spoon any remaining foam on top. Garnish with a lemon twist, if desired.

PRETTY PINK
LEMONADE SPRITZER

Pairs well with: Melon Ball Salad Platter
(page 56), Red, White & Berries (page 75),
The Grill Master (page 64) *Makes 1 cocktail*

3 ounces pink lemonade

3 ounces lemon-flavored seltzer

2 ounces gin

1 lime wheel

Edible flowers (optional)

Fill a glass with ice. Add the lemonade and seltzer, gently stirring to combine. Slowly pour the gin into the glass. Garnish with the lime wheel and edible flowers, if using.

Switch up the cocktail with different flavored lemonades and seltzers to find your favorite combination! You can also swap out gin for tequila or vodka.

Elderflower Gin Sour
(page 170)

Pretty Pink Lemonade
Spritzer (page 170)

Vanilla
Old-Fashioned
(page 172)

Spicy Cilantro
Jalapeño Mezcal
Margarita
(page 173)

VANILLA OLD-FASHIONED

Pairs well with: Fall Harvest (page 85), Spice, Spice, Baby (page 93), Festival of De-Lights (page 126) *Makes 1 cocktail*

Vanilla Bean Simple Syrup

½ cup water

½ cup granulated sugar

2 vanilla beans, split, a pinch reserved

For the Cocktail

1 pinch vanilla bean

Pinch grated orange zest

¼ ounce Vanilla Bean Simple Syrup

2 dashes orange bitters

2 ounces bourbon

1 orange twist, for garnish (optional)

1 maraschino cherry, for garnish (optional)

1. **Make the Vanilla Bean Simple Syrup:** Add the water and sugar to a small saucepan over medium heat. Stir until the sugar has dissolved. Add the vanilla to the pot, and cook for 5 to 7 minutes. Strain into a glass jar with a fine-mesh strainer or cheesecloth. Cover tightly with a lid. Store in the fridge for up to 1 month. Makes ½ cup of simple syrup.

2. **Assemble the cocktail:** In a cocktail glass, place the reserved vanila, orange zest, vanilla simple syrup, and bitters. Gently stir together. Add the bourbon and ice and stir. Garnish an orange twist and maraschino cherry, if desired.

You can also save part of your vanilla bean pod for garnish!

SPICY CILANTRO JALAPEÑO MEZCAL MARGARITA

Pairs well with: Ultimate Taco Tuesday (page 67), Say "Cheez" (page 46), Summer Floral (page 72) *Makes 2 cocktails*

1 teaspoon habanero sugar or salt (optional)

2 tablespoons chopped fresh cilantro, plus more for garnish

1 jalapeño, seeded for less heat and diced, reserving 2 slices

Juice of 2 limes

4 ounces mezcal

2 ounces Cointreau (orange liqueur)

1 ounce agave or simple syrup

2 ounces club soda

1. If sugaring the rims of the glasses, place the habanero sugar on a small plate. Rub the rim of the cocktail glasses with a lime and lightly dip them into the sugar. Fill the glasses with ice.

2. In a cocktail shaker, muddle the cilantro, diced jalapeño, and lime juice.

3. Fill the cocktail shaker with ice. Add the mezcal, Cointreau, and agave. Shake for about 20 seconds. Strain the cocktail into the prepared glasses and top with the club soda. Garnish with cilantro and the reserved jalapeño slices.

Feel free to swap out the mezcal for your favorite tequila for a more traditional spicy margarita.

AUTUMN HARVEST PUNCH

Pairs well with: Thankful for Desserts
(page 106), Oktoberfest (page 102), Gather
Round Grazing Table (page 131) *Serves 10+*

1 gallon apple cider

3 cups bourbon of choice

2 (12-ounce) cans ginger beer

12 ounces fresh orange juice

Juice of 1 lemon

1 apple, cored and sliced

1 orange, sliced

1 blood orange, sliced

4 to 5 cinnamon sticks

3 to 4 whole star anise (optional)

4 to 5 fresh cranberries (optional)

Ground nutmeg, for garnish

1. Pour the apple cider, bourbon, ginger beer, orange juice, and lemon juice into a large punch bowl and mix well.

2. Add the apple slices, orange slices, blood orange slices, and cinnamon sticks. Add the star anise and cranberries, if using. Serve over ice and garnish with a pinch of nutmeg.

This recipe is extra special with a cinnamon-sugared rim. Mix together equal parts cinnamon and sugar on a plate. Before pouring the punch, rub the rim of the glass with an orange and lightly press the rim into the mixture.

SMOKED ROSEMARY & ROYAL RIVIERA PEAR BOURBON SPRITZER

Pairs well with: Harry & David® Gift Basket Board (page 122), Holiday Happy Hour (page 121), S'more, Please! (page 76)
Makes 1 cocktail

Pear Simple Syrup

½ cup water

½ cup granulated sugar

1 Royal Riviera® pear, diced

For the Cocktail

1½ ounces bourbon

2 ounces pear juice

1 teaspoon Pear Simple Syrup

Juice of ½ lemon

2 rosemary sprigs

4 ounces ginger ale

1 Royal Riviera® pear slice, for garnish

1. **Make the Pear Simple Syrup:** In a small saucepan over medium-high heat, combine the water, sugar, and pear. Bring to a boil, then immediately reduce the heat to low. Simmer for 10 to 15 minutes. Remove from the heat, strain out the pear chunks, and allow the syrup to come to room temperature. Strain into a glass jar with a lid and store in the fridge for up to 1 month. Makes ½ cup of simple syrup.

2. **Assemble the cocktail:** Combine the bourbon, pear juice, simple syrup, and lemon juice in a cocktail shaker. Fill with ice and shake well.

3. Carefully light 1 rosemary sprig on fire, letting it burn until some of the leaves are ash. Place on a heatproof plate, cover with a serving glass, and let it smolder for about 30 seconds.

4. Strain the cocktail into the smoky glass. Top with the ginger ale. Garnish with the pear slice and remaining rosemary sprig.

WITCH'S BREW

Pairs well with: Toil & Treats Board
(page 95) *Makes 2 cocktails*

2 ounces Midori (melon liqueur)

2 ounces vodka

1 teaspoon simple syrup

1 tablespoon lemon juice

1 (7.5-ounce) lemon-lime soda

1 maraschino cherry, for garnish (optional)

1 small dry ice cube (optional)

Combine the Midori, vodka, simple syrup, and lemon juice in a glass and stir. Add ice and top with the soda. Garnish with the cherry, if desired.

To make your drink spooky with dry ice, make the cocktail as directed above, but don't add ice or garnish. Wear gloves and use tongs to transfer a 1/2-inch to 1-inch chunk of dry ice to your drink. Allow ice to melt completely or carefully and safely remove the ice cube from glass before drinking.

DO NOT SWALLOW THE DRY ICE OR TOUCH IT WITH YOUR BARE SKIN.

MULLED WINE

Pairs well with: O Christmas Cheese!
(page 129), Thanksgiving Leftovers
(page 105), Holiday Happy Hour (page 121)
Serves 8+

2 large oranges

2 (750-ml) bottles merlot or any dry red wine

½ cup brandy

½ cup packed light brown sugar

3 cinnamon sticks

3 whole star anise

6 whole cloves

Orange slices (optional)

¼ cup fresh cranberries (optional)

1. Carefully grate about 1 teaspoon of zest from one of the oranges into a large pot or Dutch oven. Slice the orange in half crosswise and squeeze both halves into the pot. Slice the second orange in half crosswise and squeeze one half into the pot. Slice the other half into rounds and place them in the pot.

2. Add the merlot, brandy, brown sugar, cinnamon sticks, star anise, and cloves to the pot and mix together. Warm the mixture over medium heat, until it just begins to simmer, then lower the heat and cook gently for about 15 minutes.

3. Serve in mugs garnished with orange slices, cinnamon sticks from the pot, and the cranberries, if using.

Keep it affordable! You don't need expensive wine for this recipe.

BOARD SCRAPS SIMMER POT

6 cups water

Leftover orange slices or rinds,
  or 1 small navel orange, sliced

Leftover apple peel or slices, or 1 small apple, sliced

3 cinnamon sticks

3 to 4 whole cloves

3 rosemary sprigs, or 1 small pine sprig

2 thyme sprigs

2 whole star anise (optional)

In a medium saucepan over medium heat, combine the water, orange, cranberries, apple peel, cinnamon sticks, cloves, and rosemary and thyme sprigs. Add the star anise, if using. Bring to a boil, then reduce the heat to low and simmer for as long as you like, adding water as needed so that the pot does not boil dry.

Call it a zero-waste stovetop potpourri. It's all natural, a good way to use up any remaining ingredients, and can be used to fill your home with a heavenly scent any time of the year. This "recipe" is great for the fall or winter, but if you wanted something brighter and lighter for the summer, try a combo of lemon, rosemary, and vanilla!

HOPELESS
HOSTESS
APPENDIX

BOARD CARE 101

Your boards are an investment, just like any other kind of kitchen equipment. Although each type of board has slightly different instructions and considerations, taking proper care will ensure you get your money's worth–especially if you've splurged on something fancy.

Wood Boards

You might not think that a wood board requires much upkeep, but let me assure you, your wooden boards need a little TLC! Unlike plastic, ceramic, or even some stone boards, wood is prone to warping and should be hand-washed and oiled regularly. While it's not necessary to perform extensive conditioning after every use, it's a good rule of thumb to do it every 3 to 4 times you use the board to prevent it from experiencing general wear and tear. Below are some things to consider when choosing a wood board and how to care for each kind.

 ACACIA: You'll want to wash this board with warm soapy water, and then dry it with a soft cloth or let it air-dry. Protect an acacia board by using a wood conditioner that contains food-grade mineral oil.

BAMBOO: Bamboo boards can split if not taken care of properly. Wash your board in warm, all-natural soapy water after every use. Towel it dry and rub it with a soft, dry cloth with food-grade mineral oil to protect it.

CHERRY: Make sure to wash cherrywood with warm, soapy, water before drying. Then apply a food-grade mineral oil or beeswax conditioner. Store your board in a shaded place because prolonged exposure to direct sunlight can damage it.

 OLIVE: To care for this beauty, make sure to gently wash it with warm water and a mild, natural dish soap. Avoid soaking olive wood for long periods since this can weaken the wood and cause it to warp. Dry your board with a lint-free or microfiber cloth and apply a thin coat of food-grade mineral oil.

 TEAK: Consistent care for teak boards is not necessary because the wood has naturally occurring oils that protect it. This means there's no need for regular treatments or conditioners. Gently scrub your board with a sponge and hot, soapy water. I recommend using eco-friendly unscented soap.

Marble Boards

 Marble isn't hard to clean, but it's a very porous material, which means it's very easy to stain! Stay away from placing super pigmented foods like blackberries, beets, etc., directly on the surface.

If you happen to stain your board, make sure to treat it immediately. Mix together a 1 heaping tablespoon of baking soda and 1 tablespoon of water until the mixture is milky and has the texture of frosting. Let the mixture sit on the stain overnight and wash it off with a sponge and warm, soapy water the next morning. If that doesn't work, try swapping the water for hydrogen peroxide and follow the same steps.

Slate Boards

 Warm, soapy water is all you need to keep slate boards looking perfect time and time again.

A BOARD FOR ALL OCCASIONS QUICK GUIDE

This book has a snack board for any occasion, time restraint, dietary need, or general vibe. These lists are not all-encompassing, but they should give you enough ideas to get started.

Under 20 Minutes

Celebrations

No Cooking Required

Under $40

Meat-Free

Kid-Friendly

Breakfast & Brunch

Easy Weeknight Meals

Impress Your Guests

BOARDS ON THE GO

Heading to a party? One of the best things about snack boards is that there's no need to worry about keeping your dish hot or things sloshing around in the back seat. Have you ever had a crockpot of buffalo chicken dip topple over your seat and onto your floor? I have–it stinks, literally and figuratively.

There are a few spreads that travel particularly well (and can usually withstand even the most overzealous driver), like the Spring Floral board (page 53), Taste of the Mediterranean (page 35), Red, White & Berries (page 75), and Toil & Treats (page 95). These boards have lifted edges to keep the food in place, which is perfect when you're on the move. Otherwise, there a few tips and tricks I've learned over the years.

PICK A SECURE SURFACE. A board with raised edges keeps things tight and protected. You could also pack everything in a reusable container with a lid, or something disposable like a brown bakery box or aluminum pan. Check out my Winery Tour To-Go Box (page 71) to see how I used a disposable box for a day filled with cheese and sipping grapes with my girlfriends.

KEEP YOUR JAMS AND DIPS IN CLOSED CONTAINERS. Look for miniature-size jam or honey jars that come with a lid–these will not only protect from spills, but they'll also avoid adding excess weight to your board. I'm usually able to find small, two-ounce jars of jam in the specialty cheese section of my local grocery store, but you can also get small jars online or in craft stores and fill them with whatever you need.

SELECT HARDY FRUITS AND VEGETABLES. I recommend staying away from produce that will wilt or brown quickly or can be easily smushed, like apples, pears, raspberries, and avocados. I've found that grapes, strawberries, blackberries, citrus slices, sugar snap peas, carrots, and cherry tomatoes travel particularly well.

SERVE YOUR CRACKERS ON THE SIDE. To avoid crackers getting soggy from freshly washed produce or possibly breaking in transit, bring your crackers in the boxes they come in or separate sturdy containers. This also prevents them from getting soft if you need to pop the board in the fridge to chill before serving. If you leave crackers, bread, or other crunchy items like nuts, pretzels, etc., in the fridge for too long, the moisture can negatively affect their crunchy texture.

WRAP TIGHTLY! Not only will cling wrap ensure that everything stays, but the taste and texture of the ingredients on the board will be preserved. I like Glad Press'n Seal because it's airtight and seals well to most surfaces. If you're packing your food in a box, tape the lid closed and double-tie it with twine to keep things intact.

KEEP THINGS COOL. If you're making a trip anywhere farther than 30 to 40 minutes away, I suggest packing your board in a thermal cooler bag with an ice pack or two. This will make sure that your softer cheeses don't begin to melt and your charcuterie and produce remain at safe temperatures to eat.

ELEVATE YOUR PRESENTATION

Once you've mastered the basics of the board, there are so many ways to get creative and really bring your presentation to a whole new level. These small tweaks not only make your board look more inviting, but they also add an unexpected artistic element that will surprise and delight your guests.

SLICE & STYLE YOUR CHEESE

Your cheese can take up a large portion of your board, so taking steps to jazz up its presentation or make your slices neat and clean can make a huge impact on your spread. I've also found that having cheeses sliced or crumbled encourages people to dig in. Here are the most common techniques I use on my boards.

Short Wedge
(Manchego, Aged Goat)

Cut thin, triangular slices by pressing firmly on your knife and cutting straight down. Use a sharp knife since the waxy rinds on these cheeses can make for a more challenging cut.

Log
(Goat)

Using a wire slicer, cut perpendicular along the log to create coin-shaped slices. To make slicing a bit easier, put your cheese in the freezer for 5 minutes. This creates a firmer texture that's easier to slice and also reduces the chance of crumbling.

Rounds

(Brie, Camembert, Humboldt Fog)

Slice these larger rounds into small wedges using a sharp knife or wire slicer. Cut the round in half and continue until you reach your desired size. They should look like little slices of pie!

Square or Rectangular Blocks

(Cheddar, Parmigianino Reggiano, Feta)

There are many ways you can slice blocks of cheese. The easiest ways are to simply cut thin slices or dice it. To dice, place the block on its slide and slice it in half. Cut each half lengthwise into thirds. Then rotate and slice horizontally to create cubes.

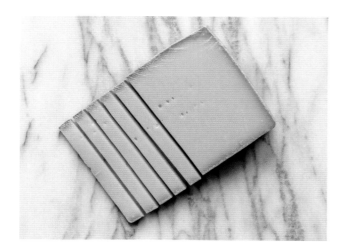

Long Wedge

(Alpine, Gouda)

Starting at the tip of the cheese opposite of the rind, make horizontal cuts. As you move closer to the rind, the slices will get thicker, and you can cut them in half or in thirds to create smaller pieces.

Shapes

(Brie, Cheddar, Manchego)

I love to make my board as festive as can be, and using cookie cutters can play up the holidays or bring home a theme. They work great with mozzarella, Brie, cheddar, Manchego—the list goes on. As long as you're not using super hard, aged cheese, you should be able to push the cookie cutter through. The best part is you can use the shape itself or fill the cutout with your favorite spread.

Rustic Crumble

(Cheddar, Feta, Parmigianino Reggiano)

One of my favorite ways to style cheese is to crumble it. Take a butter knife and press the tip into the cheese. Pull the knife backward, which should create a small, crumbly piece. You can repeat this until you have as many crumbles as you want.

Floral Cheese

(Goat, Boursin)

Place any soft cheese on a piece of plastic wrap. Decorate with edible flowers, lightly pressing them into the cheese. If you're having trouble getting the flowers to stick, try putting a little water on the cheese before applying. Wrap the plastic wrap around the cheese and apply pressure. Refrigerate for about 20 minutes until firm.

SHOW OFF YOUR CHARCUTERIE

Folding and slicing your charcuterie is a great way to add texture, dimension, and visual interest to your board. Here are some of my go-to techniques.

Single Slice
(Hard Chorizo, Pepperoni, Salami)

This easy technique is mostly used for hard charcuterie. All you have to do is thinly slice it with a sharp knife and layer the pieces onto the board.

Quarter Fold
(Genoa Salami, Soppressata)

This fold is great if you want to add height to your board since it allows you to stand the charcuterie upright. Fold the slice in half and then in half again to make a triangle.

Half Fold
(Coppa, Finocchiona Salami)

Fold smaller slices of charcuterie in half before layering them onto the board. This creates dimension without a ton of bulk.

Roll

(Mortadella, Soppressata)

Not only can you create height and dimension by rolling your charcuterie, but the shape is also perfect for grabbing from the board without much fuss. Simply roll the charcuterie into a tube, and give it a tiny pinch so it stays together. You can even roll your meats around your cheeses for an even more delicious bite.

Ribbon Fold

(Bresaola, Prosciutto)

This technique is my personal favorite! I think it looks the most interesting on a board and is pretty simple to master. First, fold the charcuterie in half. Then, holding both corners of the fold, push inward from both sides to create an S shape. You can ribbon your charcuterie from one side of the board to the other for a showstopping presentation.

If you're using prosciutto, the technique is a bit different. Lay one side of the slice on the board. Pick up the meat from one side and gently move your hand back and forth to create layers or a ribbon effect. The fat ribbon should be facing upward when you plate.

Charcuterie Rose

(Genoa Salami, Soppressata)

The most romantic charcuterie is also a great way to get a lot of charcuterie on the board without taking up a ton of space. To do this, layer 5 to 6 slices of meat in a row, overlapping each piece slightly. Cut the row in half lengthwise so you'll have 2 rows of half circles. Pick a row, and starting on one side, roll the slices until they form a small, tight-rolled cylinder. This will be the rose center.

Add the remaining half circles to the center roll one at a time, with each piece slightly overlapping the last. These are the petals. Use as many as needed to make the charcuterie rose of your dreams. Secure with toothpicks at the base or place the rose in a ramekin.

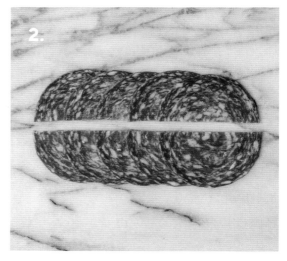

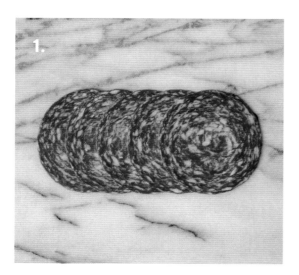

DRESS UP YOUR DIPS

Here are some of my favorite ways to keep my dips from looking like a big blob in the middle of the board.

Swoosh

Using a large serving spoon, place the tip in the center of your dip, and in one smooth motion, push the spoon down and rotate it slightly while you spin the bowl in the opposite direction.

Garnish

Since the garnish will most likely be mixed into your dip and eaten, it should do two things: elevate the flavor and the appearance. You can use fresh herbs, spices, edible flowers, chopped fruits and veggies, sauces and oils, or crunchy toppings. Just make sure whatever you add is relevant for the dip or the items on the board. I love topping my hummus with Crispy Chickpeas (page 144) and a pinch of paprika.

Rehome

If you're using store-bought dips like a bruschetta or muffuletta salad, be sure to remove them from their original container and place them in a small bowl or ramekin. This gives off the look of a homemade dip and also gives the board a uniform appearance. You can save any remaining dip in the fridge and refill your ramekin as needed.

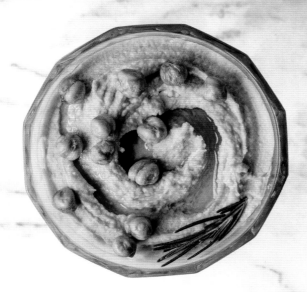

GET CREATIVE WITH YOUR CARBS & CRACKERS

A separate carb board is great when you're hosting a large group and there isn't enough space on the board or when you'd just like to offer more options for your guests. I like to include different textures, flavors, and dietary offerings so there's something for everyone. There is no wrong way to plate your crackers!

Fanning

On this board, I use a technique called fanning. Building from the center board, I fan out the breads and crackers by placing one on top of the other and keeping them tighter in the center than on the outside. This creates a really organized, clean look so that guests can clearly see each cracker. I try to separate crackers or carbs that look similar in color and shape so that there is variety across the board.

SPIFFY UP YOUR SPREAD

While your snacks are certainly the most delicious part of the presentation, there are other small (inedible) additions that can make a big impact. Creating an imaginative tablescape will help to pull through your theme and help create a more memorable experience for your guests. Make the table your canvas!

Linens & Tablecloths

Well-placed and artistically folded linens will guide your guests around the table. Choose a material that complements the food you're serving, whether that be culturally driven or motivated by your overall vision. Not only do they make your clean up easier (don't get me started on the dreaded honey drizzle across your table), but it also adds shape and dimension to your artful display of food and completes the story.

Greenery

Fresh flowers and greenery will add a lively dimension to any spread. There are so many options to choose from depending on the time of year. Around holidays you can use traditional Christmas foliage like cedar, pine, or juniper, or at the first sight of warmth in the spring choose some silver-dollar eucalyptus, tulips or baby's breath. Look to nature to bring your table to life!

Candles

Add the simple touch of unscented candlelight! It's affordable and creates a calming, elevated atmosphere. Scented candles are fine, too, but just be sure you don't have too many competing smells that could impact the taste of your food. If you're looking to add an additional pop of color, candles can really tie a tablescape together and emphasize your theme or color scheme.

Let your personality shine!

This part of the process should be—purely and simply—fun! Use unexpected patterns, antique cocktail glasses and serving utensils, throw a couple walnuts on the table for the hell of it . . . As I've said all along, treat each board like an art project and let your imagination take the lead.

DO IT FOR THE 'GRAM!

You've worked hard to create your board, so make it known! These are a few of my insider tips to capture the perfect photo of your spread for social media. (If you take away anything from this list, let it be that you should take the photo before everyone has eaten all of the snacks! Although . . . that could actually look kind of cool, too.)

FIND THE NATURAL LIGHT. This is the cardinal rule of food photography and is your key to success. Poor or harsh lighting can take away from the beauty of your food and is difficult to fix even with the best photo-editing software. Find a corner where the sun shines through your curtains and place your board on a sturdy surface to snap a pic!

ARRANGE YOUR FOOD TO TELL A STORY. Composition is key in food photography. You could always take a photo of just your board, but why stop there? Add a small ramekin off to the side with extra berries or add a few additional crackers to your table. You might even want to gently place a cheese knife directly in the cheese to make it look partially eaten. These little tweaks make the board look "lived in" and can really bring a photo to life!

USE PROPS WITH PURPOSE. Go take a second look at my Spiffy Up Your Spread section (page 196) for my tips on how you can incorporate props into your photos. Linens, utensils, greenery, and candles are all great ways to set the stage for your photo. Adding a few elements that compliment or contrast the colors in your food will bring dimension to the photo and make it more visually interesting. You're trying to a tell a story with your food and the props should help you to do that.

KEEP IT NATURAL. Don't go crazy with the edits. Let the beautiful colors of your board do all the talking! Try to use the tools of your editing software to enhance the colors of the photo without oversaturating them or muting them completely.

The goal is to enrich the photo without losing its integrity. Usually a shift in exposure, highlights/shadows, clarity, and a few color gradient changes will do. There are tons of YouTube videos that can walk you through how to do this!

PLAY WITH YOUR FOOD. Adding a human element is a simple technique that creates a sense of presence and helps to tell the story. You can show yourself grabbing a glass of wine or simply reaching for a goat cheese ball. It makes it look like you're capturing a photo from your point of view and presents your food in an interesting and engaging way.

PAIRING GUIDE

With so many options it can be daunting to find the "right" pairings with cheese (even though you really can't go wrong, in my opinion). Fortunately, there are some foundational guidelines to follow that can make pairing cheese with foods and beverages a piece of Brie... I mean, cake!

CHEESE TYPE	CHEESE NAME	BREAD & CRACKERS	FRUITS & VEGGIES	ALCOHOL	OTHER INGREDIENTS
Fresh	Burrata	Toasted ciabatta, crusty artisan bread	Heirloom tomatoes, roasted red peppers, grilled vegetables, peaches	Pinot grigio, light, high-acid white wine	EVOO, balsamic vinegar/glaze, fresh herbs
	Feta	Pita bread, crostini	Roasted vegetables, olives, onions, cantaloupe, honeydew, watermelon	Belgian-style blonde ale, light, medium-bodied ale	Honey, maple syrup, fresh herbs
	Goat cheese	French baguette, crostini	Beets, fresh figs, tomatoes, pears, berries, lemons	Riesling, sweeter, aromatic white wine	Balsamic vinegar, honey
Soft-Ripened	Brie	Puff pastry, toasted bread, hardy crackers	Apples, pears, blackberries, plums, caramelized onions, cranberries	Beaujolais, acidic, light-bodied red wine	Jam, honey, cranberry sauce
	Fromager d'Affinois	Thin, herby crackers, crusty artisan bread	Pears, apples, apricots, green grapes, mushrooms	Rosé or light, crisp, refreshing blush wine	Fig spread
	Humboldt Fog	Crostini, fruity crackers	Fresh figs, pears, tart apples, citrus, mushrooms	Sauvignon Blanc or crisp, tangy white wine	Honeycomb, cherry jam
Semisoft	Fontina	Toasted bread, fruity crackers	Dates, raisins, prunes, fresh figs, roasted vegetables	Vouvray, sparkling white wine	Chocolate, quince paste
	Muenster	Sandwich bread, herby crackers	Apples, dried fruits, red grapes	Pilsner, pale lager	Mustard, butter

CHEESE TYPE	CHEESE NAME	BREAD & CRACKERS	FRUITS & VEGGIES	ALCOHOL	OTHER INGREDIENTS
	Jarlsberg	Rye bread, dark crackers	Plums, apricots, pomegranate, grapes, apples,	Chardonnay, buttery and oaky white wine	Apple butter
Semihard	Cheddar	Seeded crackers, nutty bread	Mangoes, grapes, peaches, pears, strawberries, pickled vegetables, sundried tomatoes	Hard cider, wine with a note of apples	Dijon mustard, blackberry jam, caramel
	Gouda	Whole-grain bread, hardy crackers	Apricots, cherries, dried fruits, peaches, raspberries, potatoes	French Bordeaux, full-bodied red wine	Orange marmalade or jam, mustard, sriracha
	Gruyère	Crunchy toasts, French baguette, potato chips	Grapes, melons, figs, apples, pomegranates, blueberries, tomatoes, beets	American amber ale, caramelly, malted ale	Fig jam, honey
Blue-Veined	Danish Blue	Crusty French bread, whole-grain crackers	Tart apples, tart fruits, pears, dried cranberries	Malbec, dark full-bodied red wine	Honey, blueberry-maple compote
	Gorgonzola	Pumpernickel bread, fruity crackers	Apples, oranges, grapefruit, dried cranberries, raisins, bell peppers	Imperial India Pale Ale or hoppy, full-bodied IPA	Fig jam, orange marmalade or jam
	Roquefort	Sourdough crackers, water crackers, crusty bread	Apricots (fresh or dried), apples, grapes, fresh figs, pomegranates, roasted red peppers, celery	Port, full-bodied wine with notes of fruit, spice, and chocolate	Sour cherry jam, caramelized onion spread
Hard	Parmigiano-Reggiano	Crusty Italian bread, hardy crackers	Dates, apples, strawberries, dried fruit, fennel, sautéed greens, roasted garlic	Champagne, Italian sparkling wine	Traditional Balsamic Vinegar of Modena, truffle honey
	Pecorino Romano	Sourdough bread, fruit crackers	Melons, apples, pears, plums, blackberries, cucumbers, zucchini	Chianti, dry, medium-bodied herby wine	Strawberry jam, chestnut honey
	Manchego	Corn tortillas, crusty baguettes, water crackers	Fresh figs, grapes, dates, prunes, olives sundried tomatoes, bell peppers, poblano peppers	Wheat beer or light-bodied, citrusy ale	Quince paste, chocolate

RESOURCES & VENDORS

These are a few of my go-to vendors for ingredients and home goods.

Cheese

Boursin (www.boursin.com)

Cabot Creamery (www.cabotcheese.coop)

Cowgirl Creamery (www.cowgirlcreamery.com)

Cypress Grove Creamery
 (www.cypressgrovecheese.com)

Dorothy Creamery (www.dorothyscheese.com)

Jasper Hill Farm (www.jasperhillfarm.com)

Jersey Girl Cheese (www.jerseygirlcheese.com)

Miyoko's Kitchen (www.miyokos.com)

Rogue Creamery (www.roguecreamery.com)

Roth Cheese (www.rothcheese.com)

Sartori Cheese (www.sartoricheese.com/home.html)

Somerdale (www.somerdale.com)

Tillamook (www.tillamook.com)

Vermont Creamery (www.vermontcreamery.com)

Violife (www.violifefoods.com/us)

Wisconsin Cheese (www.wisconsincheese.com)

Summit Cheese Shoppe (www.summitcheese.com)

Charcuterie

Applegate (www.applegate.com)

Boar's Head (www.boarshead.com)

Brooklyn Cured (www.brooklyncured.com)

Citterio (www.usa.citterio.com/en/home)

Columbus Craft Meats
 (www.columbuscraftmeats.com)

Grocery

Kings Food Markets (www.kingsfoodmarkets.com)

Morristown Farmers Market (10 Wilmot St,
 Morristown, NJ 07960)

Trader Joe's (www.traderjoes.com)

Wegmans Food Market (www.wegmans.com)

Whole Foods Market (www.wholefoodsmarket.com)

Crackers & Bread

Firehook Crackers
 (www.mediterraneancrackers.com)

Lesley Stowe (www.lesleystowe.com/us)

Mary's Gone Crackers
 (www.marysgonecrackers.com)

Rustic Bakery (www.rusticbakery.com)

Edible Flowers & Herbs

Gourmet Sweet Botanicals
 (www.gourmetsweetbotanicals.com)

Jams & Honey

Bon Maman (www.bonnemaman.us)

Dalmatia Spreads (www.dalmatiaspreads.com)

Divina (www.divinamarket.com)

Heirloom Acre Honey
 (www.heirloomacrehoney.com)

Mike's Hot Honey (www.mikeshothoney.com)

Online Retailers

Harry & David (www.harryanddavid.com)

Home Goods

Crate & Barrel (www.crateandbarrel.com)

HomeSense (www.us.homesense.com)

Pottery Barn (www.potterybarn.com)

Target (www.target.com)

West Elm (www.westelm.com)

Williams Sonoma (www.williams-sonoma.com)

ACKNOWLEDGMENTS

Where do I begin? I'm eternally grateful for each and every person who has joined me on this cheesy journey that culminated in the creation of this beautiful book.

First and foremost, I'd like to thank my parents, who believed in me when I didn't believe in myself, and who taught me that flour was, in fact, *not* a good substitute for powdered sugar on brownies. Without you, who knows what would have been on these boards.

To my boyfriend, Chase, whose unwavering support, positivity, and all-encompassing love kept me going even when I thought I couldn't.

To my sister, Victoria, who inspires me endlessly with her creative vision and attention to detail. I'm so grateful to have had you as my sounding board.

To my friends and extended family, for always expressing your love and support in every possible way and for your patience as I missed gatherings and events to write this book.

Thank you to my incredible team at Gibbs Smith, for seeing the potential in me and giving me all the support I could possibly need to make this dream a reality. Thank you to my editor, Gleni Bartels, whose vision and pure talent truly made this book come to life. Thank you to my art and design team, Ryan Thomann, Gavin Motnyk, and Virginia Snow.

Last, but certainly not least, thank you to the cheese and charcuterie board community and my social media followers for your continued support and encouragement, but most importantly for your friendship. I wouldn't be here without all of you.

Oops . . . and I can't forget my sweet Minvera (Minnie) for letting me ruffle her floof whenever I felt overwhelmed and for eating all the cheese crumbs off the floor so I didn't need to vacuum.

INDEX

METRIC CONVERSION CHART

Volume Measurements		Weight Measurements		Temperature	
U.S.	Metric	U.S.	Metric	Fahrenheit	Celsius
1 teaspoon	5 ml	½ ounce	15 g	250	120
1 tablespoon	15 ml	1 ounce	30 g	300	150
¼ cup	60 ml	3 ounces	80 g	325	160
⅓ cup	80 ml	4 ounces	115 g	350	175
½ cup	125 ml	8 ounces	225 g	375	190
⅔ cup	160 ml	12 ounces	340 g	400	200
¾ cup	180 ml	1 pound	450 g	425	220
1 cup	250 ml	2 ¼ pounds	1 kg	450	230

Olivia Carney is a New Jersey-based food influencer and content creator. She daylights as a marketing director for a global healthcare company and is currently pursuing a master's degree in business administration from Pennsylvania State University. As the founder of a community for charcuterie and snack board lovers across the globe, her mission is to share her passion for food boards in a way that encourages creativity and connectedness with loved ones. She's had the pleasure of partnering with brands such as Harry & David®, Pottery Barn®, and Marshalls, among others, and has been featured in *Gotham* magazine, *Coastal Style* magazine, and PopSugar. She was born in Raleigh, North Carolina, and currently resides in North Jersey.